ISRAEL,
SERVANT OF GOD

ISRAEL,
SERVANT OF GOD

MICHEL REMAUD

With a Preface by Fadiev Lovsky

Translated by
Margaret Ginzburg and Nicole François

T&T CLARK
A Continuum imprint
LONDON • NEW YORK

T&T CLARK LTD
A Continuum imprint

The Tower Building   370 Lexington Avenue
11 York Road   New York 10017-6503
London SE1 7NX, UK   USA

www.continuumbooks.com

Authorized English translation of Michel Remaud,
Israel Serviteur de Dieu
First Published Cerf, Collection "Theologies", Paris 1983

This translation taken from 2nd edition CCEJ-Tatisbonne, 1996
Copyright © Michel Remaud c/o Margaret Ginzburg

English language copyright © T&T Clark Ltd, 2003

British Library Cataloguing-in-Publication Data
A catalogue record for this book is available from the British Library

ISBN 0 567 08880 4 (paperback)
0 567 08898 7 (hardback)

Typeset by BookEns Ltd, Royston, Herts
Printed and bound in Great Britain by
Bookcraft, Midsomer Norton

Contents

Foreword to the Second Edition

This book has been re-edited in response to a large number of requests.

There are several reasons why it might have been worthwhile to take advantage of this second edition to revise the work extensively. Since 1983, the date of the first appearance of the first edition of this book, Jewish–Christian relations have been marked by events of importance in one way or other: the visit of John Paul II to the synagogue in Rome, the affair of the Carmelite monastery at Auschwitz, publication of the Roman 'Notes' on Jews and Judaism in preaching and catechesis, recognition of the State of Israel by the Holy See ... In parallel, Christian thinking has progressed over these past thirteen years so that the literature on the subject has been enriched. The first chapter of the book had appeared in the *Nouvelle Revue Théologique* six years earlier; it was an article of its time which could serve as an introduction to the whole work though, even then, the theme might have deserved to be studied far more deeply.

Updating the book to the extent required to take all this into account would have required it to be entirely rewritten and would have ended by turning this second edition into a new book. I have, therefore, decided to republish it in a form similar to that in which it is known and cited in bibliographies. Readers interested in the subject will know where to find the necessary complementary literature for themselves.[1] Besides,

---

[1] The most recent work on our subject in French is *Ecouter Israël* (*Listening to Israel*), by Dominique Cerbelaud (Théologies; Paris: Cerf, 1995). A large number of bibliographic references will be found there. Concerning the subject of the second part, special mention should be made of Jean Dujardin's reflections, unfortunately insufficiently known, on the Shoah. I have myself extended some of the reflections in the present work in a commentary on the Roman 'Notes' of 1985 entitled *Juifs et chrétiens, un nouveau regard* (*Jews and*

there has been no change in the view I have taken in the area of the principal theme of this book as demonstrated by the actual plan of the work: the second chapter of Part 2 constituting the centrepiece, is entitled 'Unveiling'. The middle part of this chapter, echoed by the title of the book, deals with the identity and election of Israel. Christians have for too long remained blind and 'hardened' to this reality; the time has come for them to recognize the identity of the chosen people.

The principal criticism made to me at the time that the book first appeared was that I had not tackled the subject of the Land of Israel. This omission was to be explained by the conditions under which the work had come into being. It consisted of writings that had been composed under varying circumstances; I assembled them into a single volume without intending to compose a treatise.[2] In order to address this, I have added an appendix consisting of a brief commentary on the recognition

---

cont.

Christians: a new look) (Coopérative de l'enseignement religieux, 8, Rue de la Ville l'Evêque, Paris VIIIè, 1985) and also in a course given at the Faculty of Theology of Lyon in 1986 of which a summary entitled 'La rencontre du judaïsme, problème ecclésiologique' was published in the journal *Unité chrétienne* 88 (November 1987). This is not the place to supply a bibliography on Rom. 9–11. Reference may be made to Jean-Noël Aletti, *Comment Dieu est-il juste? (How is God just?)* (Paris: Seuil, 1991). (Bibliography on pp. 269–77.) Books in English include E. Fisher and L. Klenicki: *In Our Time: the Flowering of Jewish–Catholic Dialogue* (New York: Paulist/Stimulus Press, 1990); J. Pawlikowski, *Jesus and the Theology of Israel* (Wilmington, DE: Michael Glazier, 1989); M. Shermis and A. Zannoni (eds), *Introduction to Jewish–Christian Relations* (New York: Paulist Press, 1991); Clark M. Williamson, *A Guest in the House of Israel: Post-Holocaust Church Theology* (Louisville, KY: Westminster/John Knox Press, 1993).

[2] Chapter 1 ('The Election of the Jewish People') was published in *Nouvelle Revue Théologique*, (July–August, 1977) under the title 'Réflexions sur la permanence d'Israël'. Chapter 2 ('The Servant: Jesus and Israel') was published in *Nouvelle Revue Théologique* (September–October 1981). The second and third parts ('On the Shoah' and 'Facing Israel') include the contents of two series of lectures given at the Ratisbonne Centre in Jerusalem in 1981. The Appendix, 'People, Land and State', consists of a text written for the Italian journal *Qol* and slightly modified.

of the State of Israel by the Holy See. It will be obvious to the reader that this is a preliminary draft concerning a subject on which Christian thought is as yet hesitant in the extreme, although the issue will inevitably have to be taken into account in the not too distant future.[3]

---

[3] See ch. VIII 'Israël et sa terre', in Michel Remaud, *Chrétiens et Juifs entre le passé et l'avenir* (Brussels: Editions Lessius, 2000).

Preface

Christians have approached Jews, their spirituality and their destiny in several ways. When we followed the path of apologetics, we succeeded only in being ever further distanced from the people of Israel. When we reasoned from the point of view of the history of religions, the results were almost always very thin, not to say disquietingly self-justifying. When we claim that we are being guided by current events, taking social and political situations into account, we find ourselves constrained, twenty or thirty years later, to rub our eyes in astonishment at the sad results of our own unconscious short-sightedness. In this respect, I know of no better example than the analysis of Vladimir Soloviev at the end of the last century; spiritually so admirable, its practical conclusions became obsolescent under the pressure of events. During the past thirty years the U-turns of certain Christians with regard to the Jews have had the same cause: a methodology which is more to blame than their inconsistency and of which they themselves are the victims.

That is why the most important and decisive contribution of the text of Vatican II on the Jews is to be found in its first few words: 'As this sacred Synod searches into the mystery of the Church, it recalls the spiritual bond linking the people of the New Covenant with Abraham's stock.' As a Christian of the Reformed Church, I am fully at one with Michel Remaud in what he says about this Declaration of the Council. It seems to me to be of the greatest ecumenical value because it affirms that only by starting from what we are can we understand and approach others. Moving from the psychological level to the spiritual domain, it is even more the case that what enables us to encounter the identity of others is our own identity. When we are dealing with the people of Israel, made by God to be bearer and martyr – witness to revelation, we who are another people discover as we search deep into ourselves that we have more in common with the Jews than any other people does.

Consequently, Jews and Christians must approach each other, not from the point of view of current events, nor out of their own subjectivities even if these subjectivities are better disposed to each other now than in the past. There is a danger that our feelings may hide the disposition that God would like to see reigning in our hearts. The only love that lasts is the one sown in us by God, not the love which we think we create within ourselves and then accord to others. Unfortunately, we Christians have an all too harsh and melancholy experience of that sort of love, which we have inflicted on each other as well as on the Jews. At the risk of using language that is unfashionable, though echoed in the Declaration of the Council, I believe that it is in our election as Christians that we can discover the election of the people of Israel. In this sense, if the sociological, political and national reflections of Soloviev concerning the Jews living among Orthodox Russians and Catholic Poles in the context of the events of 1884 were rash and proved to be ultimately erroneous, his central intuition remains fully valid: the 'Jewish question', as it used to be called, is first of all a 'Christian question'. The only possible spiritual path on which Christians can encounter the Jews and discern the mystery of Israel is the path of investigation into the mystery of the Church. (I believe – though it is not for me to decide – that the Jews can only discover the Church and Christians, and probably also Islam and the Muslims, by studying the identity and vocation of the people of Sinai.)

If such is the case, the reader will be grateful to Michel Remaud for his courageous and innovative pages on Christian tradition, which has such questionable aspects as far as Jews are concerned. We cannot allow ourselves an easy disavowal of our terrible Christian past but we must attempt to understand it and discern the elements of truth, the signs (however ambiguous) of faithfulness, and the reasons why we went astray, in order to take responsibility for the errors, to suffer for them and consequently not to repeat them. It is because Christians have not understood or accepted the relationship that God maintains between the Church and the people of Israel and perhaps also, because they have had a confused awareness of this privileged relationship without accepting it, that their attitude to the Jews and their traditional thinking about the Jews have been so hard and so scandalous.

The time has come, late though it may be, when the Church must accept to have a single viewpoint on the people of Israel: that which God assigns to the Church when she understands herself in terms of her identity as the body of Jesus Christ. This viewpoint cannot depend on the state of the world nor on the attitudes of Jews themselves, but on the 'mystery' which reveals to the Church her own nature as willed by God. The task of the Church is to adopt this position and abandon the ivory towers from which she has been in the habit of handing down blame and withering judgements.

'Searching into the mystery of the Church ...', the Council did not say: 'Examining the mystery of the Church', still less: 'Studying the mystery of the Church'. The Council's happy choice of phrase is very significant because a mystery cannot be stated, studied or explained. It is searched into through meditation and prayer, and is discerned by faith in the same way that, according to St Paul, the body of the Lord must be discerned in the sacrament. Michel Remaud's essay fulfils the need to discern how the mystery of the Church of Jesus the Servant leads to another mystery of a different and yet conjoint nature. This essay has all the qualities of a serious theological work: it is of the highest importance that what we, in the Church, write or say about the Jews should be the result of rigorous research. But that is not enough. It must also be the fruit of spiritual intuition, the outcome of much labour performed in prayer. As much as a work of theology, *Israel, Servant of God* is to be read as a meditation searching into the mysteries of the Church and of Israel.

The scrutiny of a mystery does not distance us from other human beings. On the contrary: in denouncing the facile injustice of our expressions of opinion about Jews, Michel Remaud has put his finger on one of the reasons for this attitude; instead of thinking of Jewish women, Jewish men, Jewish communities and Jewish suffering, we have substituted for them a theological or ethical category, not to say social or political, to serve as a foil for the development of our arguments. But the Christian who searches into a mystery in spiritual meditation (and not in a state of intellectual euphoria) can no longer think in antitheses. He does not let himself be trapped inside a dilemma on the subject of the identification of the suffering Servant. He discovers that in each of the mysteries on which the New Testament calls him to meditate, God acts by love and in love. Searching into the mystery of the Church, the Christian encounters the Jewish people in the love of Christ for his people, which St Paul shared as he wrote in unforgettable and yet forgotten terms to the Romans.

Antitheses drive apart by committing the error of opposing the old to the new and tearing them apart; meditation brings close, rooting the new in the old, discerning the seed and the sap of the new in that which had been prepared to be fulfilled and renewed without being abolished. Spiritual meditation carried out in a loving spirit can dare to say in love what a prudent attitude not informed by prayer would tell us to keep silent. I see the proof of this in the humble boldness of Michel Remaud as he encounters the still unhealed trauma of the Jews caused by the Shoah. He dares to enter the zone of silence into which not even the Jews themselves, and still less the Christians, have wanted to penetrate. He can speak about the ever-present suffering of the Jews because he has searched into and meditated on the suffering of the Servant.

To conclude, I would like to underline one particular saying of Michel Remaud: 'Judaism is not anterior to Jesus; rather it is interior to him.'[1] It is not the task of the writer of a preface to summarize the full contents of a book and so I refer the reader

---

[1] In French: 'Le judaïsme n'est pas antérieur à Jésus, il lui est intérieur.'

to this intuition. If there is nothing unexpected in meeting Jesus when we search into the mystery of his Church, what is amazing is that in meeting Jesus, we discover his Jewishness; this very fact, which exposes and condemns our exegetical and Christological deviations, ought to spur us to conversion. Then, at last we shall eventually come to understand our fraternal relationship with the people in which, in obedience to his Father, he took flesh.

F. Lovsky

Introduction

Underlying the different studies composing this book, we find a double question: what is the significance of the existence of the Jewish people for Christian faith? How is it, that after twenty centuries of Christianity, the question can seem to be a new one?

Admittedly, the newness is relative. Twelve years before this book was first published, F. Lovsky in 'The rift of absence'[1] dealt with these questions at far greater length than the present work has done. More recently, English readers have had access to a very important work, *Tractate on the Jews* by Franz Mussner,[2] not to mention the many colloquia and conferences held and articles published in the recent past. But when the Second Vatican Council wanted to deal with Judaism, it did not find in the Christian heritage any vocabulary such as would enable it to speak even benevolently, let alone warmly, about the people from which Christianity originates. This relative poverty of the Christian tradition on the people from which the Church was born raises a serious question, but it is unable to furnish the material from which an answer might be construed.

Contemporary research, therefore, has in large measure to take the form of working hypotheses. This book has the ambition not so much of pronouncing definitive statements or theses as of formulating the questions that the encounter with the Jewish people raises for Christian faith. Care must be taken, in reading, not to treat silences as denials or questions as conclusions.

---

[1] F. Lovsky, *La déchirure de l'absence* (*The Rift of Absence. Essay on the Relationship between the Church of Christ and the People of Israel*), in French. (Diaspora; Paris: Calmann-Lévy, 1971).

[2] Franz Mussner, *Tractate on the Jews: The Significance of Judaism for Christian Faith* (translated from German and with a Foreword by Leonard Swidler; Philadelphia: Fortress Press; London: SPCK, 1984).

Having said that, we are not reduced solely to hypotheses; the following pages also have the aim of leading Christians to rediscover certain evidence and draw the consequences of a few truths that are too easily repressed or overlooked.

Since the shock of Hitler's attempt to annihilate the Jewish people, the Churches have been engaged in a movement of recognition of this Judaism that is the very source of their being. Hence, it is all the more necessary to conduct basic research on the links that have never ceased to connect the Church to the Jewish people. May this study contribute to this work.

PART 1

The Faithfulness of Israel

The Election of the Jewish People

Every Christian has seen illustrations of Saul on the road to Damascus falling off his horse. There have been countless iconographic representations of the persecutor falling from his mount in contexts varying from the stained-glass windows of our churches to manuals of catechism. The horse has been an essential accessory of all this imagery. Interesting attempts have even been made by a theologian of not inconsiderable stature to use the episode as a basis for developing a theology of falls from horseback. In fact, one may search the texts in vain for any mention of such an animal; we are simply told that Saul was struck to the ground. As to the horse, it is a product of Christian imagination which naturally makes up for the silence of the text because it seems obvious that Saul could not possibly have travelled on foot.[1]

This harmless example illustrates the potentially serious danger of accepting as indisputable truth certain ideas never in fact to be found in Scripture. They seem self-evident because they are linked to theological ideas that are meant to appear – though mistakenly – incontrovertible and therefore definitive.

This danger is displayed in a particularly acute manner when thought is given to the vocation of the Jewish people. For instance, it is well known that the Church calls herself the 'New Israel', and it is regrettable that Vatican II itself made use of this expression. Now traditional in theology but nowhere to

---

[1] Certain details of the text do, however, seem to suggest that he did (Acts 9.8; 22.11).

be found in the New Testament,[2] it gives the impression that
the Church has taken the place of Israel, so that from the
theological point of view Israel no longer exists. Such a
simplistic position, pushed to extremes, contradicts more
balanced texts found in the New Testament.[3] A replacement
theology of this sort is inadequate because it prevents the
Church from defining her relationship to the Jewish people at
the very time when she is showing a willingness to enter into
and pursue a dialogue with it. Fresh attempts seem increasingly
necessary, therefore, to consider new approaches to the
problem of the relationship between the Jews and the Gentiles,
in terms of a reading of Scripture devoid of any superfluous
preconceptions. As it happens, such approaches have already
been recommended by the Vatican Commission for Religious
Relations with the Jews.[4]

This task has been rendered even more urgent by one
particular aspect of contemporary Jewish life, the return of a
part of the Jewish people to the Land of its ancestors. The
renewed interest which quite a number of Christians have been
demonstrating in everything concerning Jewish existence can
no doubt be explained in large part by the Return, by the events

---

[2] Dogmatic Constitution *Lumen Gentium* on the Church chap. 2, n. 9, §3.
Ad Gentes decree on the missionary activity of the Church, chap. 1, n. 5.

[3] In particular Rom. 9–11 and Eph. 2–3.

[4] Guidelines and Suggestions for Implementing the Conciliar Declaration
Nostra Aetate no. 4 (1 December 1974), §III, text in *Stepping Stones to Further
Jewish–Christian Relations*, Helga Croner (ed.), London and New York:
Stimulus Books, 1977). This article was written at the time of the meeting of
the International Committee for Liaison between Catholics and Jews (Venice,
28–30 March 1977). Its 'official communiqué' contains extracts of the report
presented in the name of the Catholic delegation by Professor Federici. More
important than its rejection of 'proselytism' (which barely goes beyond the
Declaration of Vatican II on religious liberty) is the invitation to emphasize
from the Catholic side the 'permanence of Judaism in God's plan' and
especially the affirmation: 'In her mission to spread the knowledge of the
name of God, the Church recognizes that she is strongly linked to the task of
the Jewish people in the world'. International Catholic–Jewish Liaison
Committee, *Fifteen Years of Catholic–Jewish Dialogue, 1970–1985* (Rome:
Libreria Editrice Laterense and Vaticana, 1988).

that directly brought it about and by the resulting international situation. In their recent documents, Catholic authorities have found it prudent to abstain from making any theological judgement on the matter of the Return.[5] At the present time there can be no question of reaching any mature conclusion on the problem of the relation between the Jewish people of today and the Land. What the Return is really encouraging us to do is to do justice to the 'mysterious' nature of Jewish reality and to forestall the potential dangers arising from overly simplistic ideas. Indeed, recent statements suggest that unfortunate consequences might be drawn (no doubt not in accord with the intentions of their authors) from theologies making overconfident claims to decipher the mystery of Israel and its destiny. A few present-day theologians have been seen striving to use Scripture in order to prove the inadmissible character of Jewish claims to the Land so as to liberate the consciences of those Christians who might otherwise feel obligated by a misguided generosity to support a cause whose indefensibility these theologians claim to be able to demonstrate from the Gospels.[6]

Let us repeat that the subject of the following reflections is not the Land but a much more fundamental problem to which the Return inevitably attracts our attention, namely that of the permanence of the Jewish people and of the meaning that the Church can grant this permanence.

After showing the blind alleys which certain ways of considering the Jewish reality are bound to lead into, I then propose to give an example of another possible approach, to demonstrate that the theology of replacement is not the only one possible. Finally, I shall give consideration to the likely

---

[5] See in particular the Statement by the French Bishops' Committee for Relations with Jews, April 1973. Translated from French in Croner (ed.), *Stepping Stones,* p. 60.
[6] See for instance J. Landousies, 'Le don de la terre de Palestine' ('The Gift of the Land of Palestine'), in French, *Nouvelle Revue Théologique* (April 1976), pp. 324–36.

consequences of a renewed Christian approach to Jewish reality.

Blind Alleys

When we deal with Judaism, the idea of obsolescence often comes up. For instance, the arguments of the theologians just mentioned rely on the idea that the relation between the Jewish people and the Land belongs to an economy now past. However, it is here that difficulties arise since the existence of the Jewish people is an undoubted fact. So there arises the inevitable question as to what aspect of its existence might be outmoded because bound up with an obsolete economy, and whether the Jewish people might retain something imperishable because bound up with its Jewish identity. Of course, it could be argued that the present-day existence of the Jewish people is in itself a theological anachronism, in which case all that the Church can do is to work toward its conversion or its suppression, or else to wait patiently for its disappearance. We are inevitably led back to the question as to what meaning the Church sees in the permanence of Israel.

Christian thought has always been at a loss to assign a theological status to contemporary Jewry. The Church recognizes willingly that she owes her origin to the Jewish people[7] whom she hopes to meet at the end of history,[8] but she feels great embarrassment in placing herself in relation to the Jewish people in the present. Roughly, Christian thought, as expressed at least in current teaching, swings between two attitudes.

The first defines things Jewish in exclusively negative terms. The Jew becomes a sort of inverse image of the Christian, personifying law as opposed to grace, the letter as opposed to

---

[7] Conciliar Declaration *Nostra Aetate* on the non-Christian religions, no. 4, §2.
[8] *Nostra Aetate*, no. 4.

the spirit, flesh as opposed to spirit, particularism as opposed to universality, works as opposed to faith and fear as opposed to love ... These are the logical consequences of the basic choice that, according to this approach, makes a Jew Jewish, namely his refusal of the Gospel and his hardened lack of faith. Thus, the permanence of the Jewish people becomes a sort of grand parable of sin. It is easy to see the foundations of this way of thinking in the New Testament, and that merely intensifies the embarrassment of Christians when they become aware that a portrait of this sort is simply a caricature.

If they recognize how little the negative description just given has to do with actual reality, Christians will therefore prefer to adopt another attitude which consists in recognizing 'values' in Judaism – Judaism can hardly have exclusive claims to these since all values are supposed to belong as of right to the Church in virtue of her catholicity. Jews are now presented as people of good faith who have lost their way and who live a religious life worthy of respect although they are in a situation of objective error. According to this hypothesis, Judaism is assigned the status of a non-Christian religion, a status that takes no account of its specific nature nor of its original situation relative to the Church. It is worthy of note that Christians adopting this attitude rarely accept Judaism according to its own self-definition, but redefine it on their own initiative and according to their own criteria. Current ecclesiastical discourse on the 'Jewish religion' often actually manages to talk about Judaism without mentioning the Covenants, the Promises, the Land, messianic hopes or even ... the Jewish people.

In both cases Christians avoid positive interpretations of Jewish existence, whether considering the Jews as a people, or with reference to the Covenant. This leads us to a crucial question: can the Church, without self-betrayal, find any positive meaning in the permanence of the *Jewish people* as such?

What Kind of Unity?

The permanence of the Jewish people appears to embrace two distinct realities which cannot be confused, although one masks the other in the eyes of Christians, since it is so difficult for us to admit that two interpretations of the same reality could possibly both be true at one and the same time.

It is undeniable that the permanence of Israel in the face of the Church does express the non-acknowledgement of Jesus as Messiah, with all the questions that arise from such an attitude.[9]

But this reality masks another, the permanence of the Jewish people as Jewish, that is to say as chosen and separated from the nations. The identity of the Jewish people goes back to the Covenant and does not stem from its attitude toward the gospel. Does the gospel demand from Israel the loss of its identity? If this be the case, but only if so, the one possible conclusion is that what makes the Jew Jewish is his refusal to acknowledge the gospel.

At first sight the answer to this question is simple: did not Paul say that Jesus has 'made the two into one entity and broken down the barrier' (Eph. 2.14)? It seems to follow that the vocation of Israel must be to dissolve into a 'new people' in which Jews and pagans become mixed into an undifferentiated whole. But is this fusion the only possible way of conceiving unity? Concerning this final point, has Scripture anything to tell us that, here again, could lead us beyond mistakenly simplistic ideas?

Concerning unity, Scripture presents us with two great paradigms, complementary rather than being superimposed on each other. First, we think of the unity of the Father and the Son which Jesus presented in his 'priestly prayer' as the type of unity that must come into being between the disciples: 'so that they may be one like us' (John 17.11). This is not fusion but

---

[9] There is no question of denying this point or even of making an abstraction of it. Here we wish to draw attention to the other aspect of Jewish permanence which almost always goes unnoticed.

rather mutual recognition and love which allow each person to retain his identity. The other paradigm is that of the unity of man and woman evoked at the beginning of Genesis (Gen. 2.24) and called upon to become the sacramental image of the union of Christ and the Church (Eph. 5.32). Here again, we see a type of unity which, far from doing away with identities, is realized in a mutual recognition where each comes to fullness in his or her own singularity.

If the unity of Jews and Gentiles is at stake in God's ultimate intervention in the history of humankind (cf. Eph. 3.1–11), if the reconciliation of the Jew and the Greek is the parable and type of every reconciliation, how can one doubt that it must be accomplished in the image of the unity of the Father and the Son, as Jesus himself requested? As for the relationship between man and woman, there are at least two indications that it sheds light on the mystery of the relationship between Israel and the nations. First, the fact that the man–woman couple is associated by St Paul with the Jew–Greek couple and both are placed on the same level (cf. Gal. 3.28). Even more important is the similarity between the expressions evoking the unity of each of these two couples: 'They become one flesh' (Gen. 2.24); 'the two become one flesh' (Eph. 5.31); 'to reconcile both of them to God in one body' (Eph. 2.16).

Pursuing this line of thought further we are led to say that the election of Israel has introduced a duality into the human species which not only has not been erased but which is not destined to be erased. It must be overcome in so far as it signifies division or hostility[10] but it constitutes the foundation of a reciprocal relationship in which Israel and the Gentiles are called to realize their vocation.

The eschatological unity which, paradoxically, only Jesus can bring about must therefore be realized in mutual love between Israel and the Gentiles. It can already be foreseen that, were this love to be realized, Jesus would be acknowledged at the same

---

[10] In the same way that Gal. 3.28 ('neither male nor female') clearly does not signify that the gospel has abolished the distinction between the sexes.

time as its enabling agent. On the pagan–Christian side, which is the only one on which we can honestly stand if we are not Jewish, the only way in which Jesus can appear to us is as the one who leads us to love the Jews and not as the one who would incite us to wipe out their identity.

This love for the Jews must be founded on a recognition of what is unique to them. It is not a case of loving them while abstracting from what defines them; they must be loved for what they are. For if Jew and Greek are equal in the Lord, this equality does not cancel out the difference which the symbolic economy of salvation has established between them.

The distinguishing mark of the Jewish people is to have been chosen to mediate the Father's gift to the Gentiles. The Church of the Gentiles cannot therefore deny Israel but must, on the contrary, recognize Israel as the people from which she originated. Recognition of this sort does not merely send us back to the Israel of former times. It is not enough to admit to a historical relationship between the Jewish people of the past and the Church of today. Israel has kept its identity throughout history; the relationship uniting it to the living Christ, just like the one which unites Christ to his Church, is not destroyed by time. We are therefore obliged to recognize Israel as the people from whom we receive Jesus Christ in order to be introduced by him into the Covenant:[11] 'salvation comes from the Jews' (John 4.22); far from making the formula obsolete, the coming of Jesus gives it its full content.

Recognition of Israel constitutes a firm refusal to dissociate Jesus from his people; it follows that our relationship to Jesus sends us back to the people with whom he is at one. Now, if the Church claims Jesus as spouse and Lord, she feels all too

---

[11] We have the experience of receiving Jesus from the Jewish people in the encounter with living Judaism. This allows us a better understanding of Jesus and of his mystery and therefore enables us to have a more intimate relationship with him. This is the most accessible, if not necessarily the most profound aspect of the fact that the Church and humanity go on receiving Jesus from Israel whether this latter is aware of it or not.

often obliged to isolate him – and herself – from the Jewish people, thereby refusing the great reconciliation accomplished on the cross. She must stop separating that which God has united, she must stop pulling Jesus away from his people, and, *a fortiori*, she must stop making him a champion in the fight against all things Jewish, for if he is no longer Jewish, he is no longer Christ. Even when glorified, he cannot be dissociated from the people whose vocation he fulfils. And the 'rejection' of Rom. 11.15 does not put an end to this relationship: it is by the first-born Son, the Servant, who is Jesus and Israel at one and the same time that God's gift comes to us.[12]

The recognition of Israel by the Gentiles is founded upon this Jewish mediation, accomplished in Jesus Christ;[13] it is related to the sacramental order and displays the gratuitous nature of salvation. The scandal that such an idea can cause must help us to understand the difficulties which others have in comprehending ideas of election and of mediation in the order of salvation. It appears scandalous to the human mind that God should choose some particular group or individual for the mediation of a grace destined for all. But any Christian tempted to refuse to admit the principle of such a mediation must ask himself how he can accept the sacramental economy, the ministerial institution and, even more radically, the unique mediation of Jesus Christ with all that came before and that follows from it.

Concrete Attitudes

We have been referring to the recognition of Israel by the pagan nations. As a matter of symmetry, it should be said that the Jewish people ought to recognize the Church of the Gentiles as that which is its issue, bone of its bone and flesh of its flesh. In

---

[12] Israel is called 'First-born son' in Exod. 4.22 and 'Servant' in Isa. 49.3.

[13] The terms 'Israel' and 'Gentiles' are used exclusively in the biblical sense.

fact the Church is not in a position to preach to Israel and, in any case, experience shows, if any such demonstration were needed, that sermonizing here falls on deaf ears. But the Church can and must behave in such a manner that recognition of this sort should not be made impossible in practice.

There follow very practical consequences in our way of relating to the Jewish people.

Let us consider a single aspect of this problem: a good number of Christians, including theologians, consider that the Church and individual Christians must differentiate themselves from Judaism by making comparisons in which, for the honour of the gospel, the superiority of all things Christian must always be maintained. Some Christians are even perturbed when they discover points of faith or religious habits in Jews which they had thought to be specifically Christian, for their sense of identity is then endangered. More generally, they do not sufficiently resist the temptation to present a rather caricatural view of the Jew in order to better display the newness of the Christian message.[14] Let us illustrate this point by two examples, very simple but revealing.

The first is anecdotal. During a Jewish–Christian meeting a rabbi makes a comment on the precept 'you ... will love your neighbour as yourself' (Lev. 19.18). The rabbi observes that since the precept does not include any limitation, it includes the obligation to love all men including strangers and enemies. At this point certain Christians reproach the rabbi for giving too broad an interpretation to the text: love of strangers and of enemies expresses the gospel ideal (and therefore logically the Jew is not bound by it). Quite independently of exegetical

---

[14] Fr. Bouyer has given a good description of this attitude: 'Modern Christians find it extraordinarily difficult to rid themselves of a view of Judaism in which everything is simply the opposite of Christianity. Dead legalism, a notion of religion based entirely on the flesh: might one not think that our apologetics need a foil in order to set the figure of Jesus in sufficient relief?' (L. Bouyer, *Le Trône de la Sagesse. Essai sur la signification du culte marial* (*The Throne of Wisdom: Essay on the Significance of the Veneration of Mary*)) in French (Paris: Cerf, 1957) p. 62.

aspects of the question, it thus appears that the Christian considers universal love to be a sort of monopoly which gives Christianity its specificity; he fears that the Jew might steal *his* charity.

The second example is a good illustration of a certain manner of referring to Judaism. A recent theological essay includes the following description of religion in the time of Jesus:

> His adversaries [those of Jesus] had no concern for the sinner or for the poor. Their concern was for the Law and its application: according to the Law, Man is made for the Sabbath, the visible symbol of the sovereignty of the Law. This was pushed so far as to favour injustice by disregarding what summed up the Old Testament revelation 'Thou shalt love the Lord thy God and thy neighbour as thyself'. 'Sin' acquires an objective role as God is obliged through His law to destroy Man: the honouring of God – for that is the aim of the Law and of religion – has become a factor favouring the contempt of Man. Serving God leads to homicide; the killers of the prophets, as of Jesus, think they are glorifying Him ... Jesus did not say that sin had to do with disobedience to laws or codes. He spoke of the proliferation of evil in other terms. He looked at it afresh by seizing it at its source whereas the religious person of his day turned God into the enemy of Man.[15]

[15] C. Duquoc, *Jésus, homme libre. Esquisse d'une christologie*, 2ᵉ éd. (*Jesus, Free Man: Sketch of a Christology*), in French (Paris: Cerf, 2nd edn, 1974), pp. 101–102. It is revealing to compare this text with that written at about the same time by a Jewish writer. Concerning the Akeda (the sacrifice of Isaac), Elie Wiesel writes: 'Let us mention in passing the role that the Akeda plays in Christianity: the menace Isaac faced is regarded as a prefiguration of the crucifixion, except that on Mount Moriah the act was not consummated, the father did not abandon his son and certainly not to death. Such is the distance between Moriah and Golgotha. In Jewish tradition death is not a means which man would use to glorify God. Every person is an end in themselves, a living eternity: no one has the right to offer another up in sacrifice, not even to God. Had Abraham killed his son, he would not have become our father and our intercessor. For the Jew every truth springs from life, not from death.

The text quoted certainly does show one of the points of disagreement between Jesus and some of his adversaries. But is that really the portrait of 'the religious person of his period'?[16] And are such contrasts needed to reveal the face of Jesus?

And since we are in this area, the desire to demonstrate the originality of Christianity by separating it off from Judaism may perhaps explain, at least in part, certain arguments advanced to support positions taken concerning the problem of the Land mentioned at the beginning. We might then have the key to a curious puzzle: in the name of the spiritual conception of salvation brought by the gospel, Jewish hopes are criticized as being too earth-centred – as if Jewish hopes were not equally spiritual – and then it is declared in the name of the incarnation that salvation is concerned with the whole of human existence and that faith must be expressed in the political arena – as if these opinions were radically new as compared to Judaism. In both cases everything takes place as if the Christian will refuse to be in the company of the Jew even when they are standing on the same ground. Independently of the particular reasons that might explain such and such a political position on the conflict in the Near East, one can discern the more or less conscious determination of Christianity to reserve for itself the

cont.
For us, the crucifixion represents a backward rather than a forward step; at the summit of Mount Moriah the living stay alive, thus marking the end of ritual murder. By invoking the Akeda we make an appeal to grace whereas throughout the length of centuries Golgotha has served as pretext for numberless massacres of fathers and of sons by the sword and by fire in the name of a so-called love'. Elie Wiesel, *Célébration biblique (Biblical Celebration)*, in French (Paris: Seuil, 1975), pp. 73–4. Do Jews and Christians have to caricature each other in order to remain distinct?

[16] Cf. L. Bouyer once more: 'One might imagine that Jesus and his teaching appeared in Palestine as if from outer space, though this conception would be based on a dangerously monophysitic view of the incarnation in which what is human is absorbed and as it were abolished in the divine. But how did it come to pass that so legalistic a religion produced a being with such faith and generosity as the Virgin of Luke?' (*Le Trône de la Sagesse*, p. 62).

discovery and practical application of a certain conception of salvation, strangely failing to see that it follows in a straight line from Old Testament conceptions. For if ever there were a dichotomy that is unbiblical, it would be one that set the material against the spiritual. And just as Jesus did not allow a choice between physical healing and the forgiveness of sins, the religious Jew does not feel himself obliged to choose between the salvation of the 'soul' and of the body. Anyone with some slight familiarity with Jewish thought knows that observance of the Torah has as its precise aim the sanctification of the whole of human existence both private and public.

These similarities between Jewish and Christian conceptions, similarities which often trouble the Christian because they appear to threaten his very identity, on the contrary allow the mutual recognition already mentioned. The attitude that consists in underlining the difference in every possible way proceeds from the undoubtedly praiseworthy desire to illuminate the pre-eminence of Jesus Christ and the newness of the gospel. (Though we have to be very careful to situate this newness where it really belongs.) But such an attitude is inadequate unless coupled with an equally strong desire to show that Jesus comes to fulfil rather than to destroy (cf. Matt. 5.17; Acts 26.22). Far from causing the Christian to contest *a priori* all Jewish attempts to express faith within the framework of everyday private and public life, the desire to emphasize the fulfilling work of Jesus can encourage the Christian to feel well disposed toward such an attitude, since his own conversion to the gospel enables him to understand the underlying intention from within. And if he feels obliged to disagree with some Jewish expression or other or with something he deems to be an act of unfaithfulness, his critique need in no way be founded on the gospel. He should even deliberately avoid taking up that kind of position because invocations of the gospel imply that he is locked up within the incommunicable, as if to say that only the disciple of Jesus Christ can see things as he sees them, so that consequently the non-Christian is excused in advance for seeing them otherwise. The Christian who feels it imperative to voice disagreement or criticism, will find common ground for an encounter with the Jew in the Law and the Prophets where both can submit to the judgement of the Word of God and understand more deeply the demands of the Covenant.

As for the Christian, he will be helped by the gospel to remember that reconciliation is brought about through the humility of the Servant rather than by the certitude of the master.

✡ ✡ ✡

The Guidelines and Suggestions of 1 December 1974 for religious relations with Judaism – a document whose caution has been specially noted – includes a far-reaching but little-noticed phrase: 'The problem of relations between Jews and Christians concerns the Church as such, since it is "when pondering her own mystery"[17] that she is confronted with the mystery of Israel. Therefore, even in areas where no Jewish communities exist, this remains an important problem.'[18]

It is not legitimate to wait for the problem to lose its urgency before starting to tackle it, because it goes to the heart of the Church's concerns. In any case, the question has become so intimately bound up with the history of salvation that there can be no thought of it ever becoming purely academic.

Anything touching the Jewish people inevitably awakens such strong feelings that it is impossible to proceed without the most extreme caution. The ideas just expressed are not claiming to substitute one synthesis for another. Tentative and fragmentary as they are, they are put forward as one example among others of ways along which future thinking might develop.

But one essential condition must be – to return to our preliminary image – that the horse be given up and that we agree to go on foot rather than try to ride on a mount that does not exist.

---

[17] Cf. below pp 109–10.

[18] Conclusion of the Guidelines and Suggestions for the application of the Conciliar Declaration *Nostra Aetate* no. 4 published by the Vatican Commission for Religious Relations with the Jews, January 1975.

2

The Servant: Jesus and Israel

Of all the theological documents promulgated by the Second Vatican Council, only the text on the Jews is without a single reference to any of the teachings of the Church, whether patristic, conciliar or pontifical.[1] As is usual for all the declarations of the Magisterium, documents of Vatican II include references to former tradition. These references vary in number from one text to another – a significant point in itself – and aim at demonstrating continuity between the tradition of the Church and the proposed teaching. The text on the Jews is the sole exception to this rule in that it refers exclusively to Scripture.[2] Even though traditional material on the subject does exist,[3] there seemed no possibility of making use of it as it stands. We shall naturally have to return to this point but for the present we need notice only that as the Council was unable to refer to any authoritative material other than the New Testament, it was obliged to consider the Jewish people in the light of the origins of the Church on the one hand, and of

---

[1] Declaration *Nostra Aetate* (on the relations of the Church with non-Christian religions), no. 4, The Jewish religion.

[2] F. Lovsky, *La Déchirure de l'absence*. (*The Rift of Absence: Essay on the Relationship between the Church of Christ and the People of Israel*), in French (Diaspora; Paris: Calmann-Lévy, 1971) p. 37.

[3] See (in particular): Marcel Simon, *Verus Israel: A Study on Relations between Christians and Jews in the Roman Empire* (translated from French by H. McKeating; New York: for the Littman Library by Oxford University Press, 1986); F. Lovsky, *Antisémitisme et mystère d'Israel* (*Antisemitism and the Mystery of Israel*) (Paris: Albin Michel, 1955); Bernard Blumenkranz, *Juifs et chrétiens dans le monde occidental (430–1096)* (*Jews and Christians in the Western World, 430–1096 C. E.*) (La Haye: Mouton, 1960).

eschatology on the other. As far as the present-day relationship between Israel and the Church is concerned, the statements of the Council are limited to generalities on universal brotherhood, the condemnation of persecution and racial discrimination without a single specifically theological pronouncement – and this concerning the people from which the Church has originated.

The only way of venturing into this no man's land of theological silence on contemporary Judaism is by suggesting hypotheses. But if the intention of starting a 'fraternal dialogue'[4] with the Jews is to be taken seriously, we cannot possibly limit ourselves to humanitarian discourse; the need to make a specifically theological pronouncement on the subject of Israel and on the relationship between the Church and the Jewish people cannot be dodged for ever.

It is therefore in the form of a hypothesis, with all the risks that this may entail, that we are led to ask whether the Church can and should recognize the Jewish people of today as possessor of the title and quality of Servant, with all the biblical background implied by this term, specifically as in the second part of the book of Isaiah.

The Servant, Israel, Jesus

From its side, Jewish tradition has constantly identified the figure of suffering Israel with the Servant. That was true a long time before what is known as the 'Holocaust', the culmination of a long history of persecution, exile and humiliation. When dispersed among the nations and considered by them as 'struck with affliction by God' (Isa. 53.4),[5] interceding for sinners (cf. Isa. 53.12) by unceasing prayer, holding in its very kenosis to

---

[4] *Nostra Aetate* no. 4.

[5] Unless otherwise indicated, biblical quotations are made from the New Jerusalem Bible.

the duty of praising God (its service: *avoda*),[6] the people of Israel has always found the key to its own destiny in Isaiah 53.[7]

On its side, Christian tradition has always from the beginning unhesitatingly answered the question asked of Philip by the eunuch of Queen Candace: 'Is the prophet referring to himself or someone else?' (Acts 8.34; cf. Matt. 8.17; Luke 22.37; John 12.38; Rom. 15.21; 1 Pet. 2.24): Jesus is the Servant whose sufferings and death justify the multitudes. There is no need to recapitulate here the history of the exegesis and theology of Isaiah 53 in Christian tradition.[8]

Even so, it is legitimate to ask whether the two interpretations are mutually exclusive. If so, the Christian would be under the obligation to choose one or the other, that is to say, the latter. Or might it be permissible, on the other hand, to accept that the mysteries of Christ and of Israel are mutually inclusive so that the two interpretations, far from being mutually exclusive, are contained within each other? If it is true, as we believe, that the Scriptures are accomplished in Jesus Christ, we may be willing to assent as well to the proposition that Christ represents a sort of crystallization of the destiny of

---

[6] The word *avoda* denotes both service and liturgical prayer. It is appropriate to recall the account of the death of Rabbi Akiba: 'When Akiba was taken out to be condemned to death it was the hour for the recitation of the Shema. His flesh was torn with combs of iron and he took on himself the yoke of the Kingdom of Heaven. His disciples said: "Master, as far as this?" He answered: "Every day I wept over this passage: *With all your soul* (that is to say:) *Even if He takes your soul*. And I would say to myself: 'When will the time come?' And now that the time has come, shall I not accomplish it?"' Talmud B. *Berakhot*, 61b.

[7] The application of Isa. 52.13–15 and 53.11–12 to Israel, now classic in Judaism, is far from being exclusive and became accepted only gradually. Rabbinical literature has applied these passages to Rabbi Akiba, to Moses, to the righteous person in general and especially to the Messiah. The application to Israel as attested in the Midrash (*Numbers Rabba*, 13.2) was worked out by Ibn Ezra in the 12th century. See A. Neubauer and S. R. Driver: *The Fifty-Third Chapter of Isaiah According to the Jewish Interpreters* (2 vols.; New York: KTAV, 1969).

[8] Cf. P.-E. Bonnard, *Le Second Isaïe, son disciple et leurs éditeurs. Isaïe 40–66*, (Etudes bibliques; Paris: Gabalda, 1972).

his people. According to this hypothesis, the two readings of Isaiah are far from being mutually exclusive; they include and at the same time illuminate and mutually confirm each other.[9]

[9] The hypothesis thus presented is unlikely to receive support from patristics, the chief preoccupation of which is to prove that Jewish hermeneutics and Christian hermeneutics concerning the situation of the Jews after Christ are mutually exclusive. (Cf. Simon, *Verus Israel*, and particularly pp. 190–2. Jewish tradition on the subject is equally polemical and apologetic. Cf. Neubauer and Driver, *Fifty-third Chapter of Isaiah*). This should encourage us, following Vatican II, not to accord to tradition an absolute authority on this subject. The question to be asked here is probably not how to use the Fathers of the Church – or how to ignore them. Neither is it to ask whether one might have the right to step over nineteen centuries of history in order to return, in this particular case, to *Scriptura sola*. It is preferable to try to explain how the Fathers came to their attitudes on Judaism and how the Church can take a fresh look at the Jewish people according to the perspective of God's designs, as revealed across the centuries, and of her growing understanding of those designs, by faith, throughout the course of a history of sin and grace.

The catastrophe that Nazism brought down on the Jewish people has had the effect of opening the eyes of many Christians to make them take a fresh look at the Jewish people. (This might be an occasion to reflect on the relationship that may exist between the event and the reading of Scripture in general.) Certain Christians are then enabled to formulate explicitly the resemblance of Israel to the suffering Servant. As an example let us quote a few sentences spoken by Karl Barth at a conference held on 23 July 1944: 'The insensate and frenetic persecution of the Jewish people is ... for us the image of this "Servant of the Eternal" that the book of Isaiah shows us as punished and sacrificed for others. Is it not the Lord Jesus Christ himself who is visible "as in a glass darkly" behind all these Jews of Germany, France, Poland and Hungary who are shot, buried alive, crammed into cattle trucks where they are stifled, or asphyxiated by gas? Are not these facts a revelation, a message, a word, a testimony from God? Is it possible that the Christian community does not see what or who is involved here? Is it possible that the Christian not fall to his knees to cry: "You carried the sins of the world, Oh Lord, have pity on us! You are there, in the shadow of a persecuted and massacred Jew, and it is you who once more are being rejected. It is your lonely death that these events again show us". In the same way that God gave up his Son for us two thousand years ago, it is again Christ stricken by the tragic fate of his brothers and sisters according to the flesh ...' (quoted by Lovsky, *Antisémitisme et mystère d'Israel*, p. 417).

On his side, Jacques Maritain (1944) wrote: 'Israel unwillingly treads the path of Calvary side by side with Christians, and these strange companions are

As a matter of fact, there is an impressive similarity, perhaps even an identity, between the historic destinies of Israel and of Christ. After Auschwitz there is no need for lengthy arguments to explain why one cannot but see a resemblance between the Jewish people and he who was 'cut off from the land of the living' (Isa. 53.8). The Shoah[10] took to extreme limits and in some way exposed the mechanisms, meaning and absurdity of an anti-Judaism at work for centuries during which the Jewish people have never ceased to live the part of the persecuted Righteous.[11] Both Jesus and Israel have lived to the extreme limit the destiny of the suffering Righteous known only to God and bearing the weight of the sin of the world. At the decisive moment both experience the silence of God, a silence in which their adversaries seem to have been proven right (cf. Ps. 22.8–9) and into which the Righteous is plunged: a situation which is 'objectively' – so to speak – that of humanity separated from God. At the decisive moment God does not intervene to save his Son from death.[12] Jesus dies, apparently abandoned by God

---

cont.
sometimes surprised to find themselves together. As in the admirable picture of Chagall, the unfortunate Jews are carried away in the great tempest of the Crucifixion without understanding what is happening to them "surrounding Christ stretched over a world that is lost". The central fact, no doubt of the greatest significance from the point of view of philosophy and of the history of human destinies, is that nowadays the passion of Israel takes more and more distinctly the form of the cross.' Jacques Maritain, 'La Passion d'Israël' ('The Passion of Israel'), in *Le mystère d'Israël et autres essais* (The Mystery of Israel and Other Essays) (Paris: Desclée de Brouwer, 1965), pp. 202–203.

[10] In Hebrew: catastrophe. Term designating genocide known incorrectly as 'holocaust'. Cf. next chapter.

[11] Refusal to allow the designation of Righteous to Israel on the grounds that not every Jew is faithful to the Covenant is as misguided as refusing to call the Church 'Holy' because of the sins of Christians. It may be appropriate here to prevent misunderstanding, and emphasize that the fact of paying special attention to Jewish suffering does not indicate that the suffering of non-Jews is less worthy of consideration but, rather, is meant to recognize that the existence of Israel, like that of Christ, has a typical significance and function which precisely throw light on all human experience.

[12] The term 'Son' is naturally used here to designate both Israel (cf. Exod. 4.22) and Jesus Christ (cf. Matt. 3.17).

in a radical trial of faith that seems to nullify the promises and prove the believer wrong. It is impossible to plumb the mystery of what Jesus went through in his death. But it would be a mistake to absorb that death too quickly into the resurrection by forgetting that it was a real death and an hour of darkness. It would be equally mistaken to trivialize the Shoah by forgetting its specific nature which consisted of the killing of the people of the Covenant. The genocide was not simply a putting to death of human beings; it was a putting to death of God in the heart of humans.[13]

Throughout this trial of faith the Servant did not cease to pray and to praise his God from the very depths of death and the absurd. Jesus died praying (Matt. 27.46–50; Luke 23.34–46, 46). Throughout the Shoah, the heart of Israel never ceased praising God and confessing its faith in him.[14]

The fact is that there is but one Servant who is at the same time Jesus and Israel. Or rather: who is Israel, whose vocation is realized in Jesus Christ without Israel being thereby divested of its identity or mission.

In Jesus Christ the Servant carried the sin of the world. He overcame the trial of the silence of God. He retained his faith while being severely tested and apparently abandoned by God.

---

[13] Cf. Elie Wiesel, *Night* (translated from French by Stella Rodway; New York: Hill and Wang, 1960).

[14] 'It has become clear that the Holocaust, that terrible sign of contradiction, brought believing Jews to display a heroic act of faith. Those who never stopped praying even through abandonment, misery and tears, who like the hero of "The Last of the Just" entered the gas chambers reciting the *Shema Israel* and those who transformed their death into a final act of self-surrender, those are truly the inheritors of Jewish wisdom. They heard the voice of the Almighty above the noise and fury, the curses and shouts of their torturers. To the very end they remained faithful to the call of *Shema Israel*. Far from being passive victims, their silence expressed *Qiddush Hashem*, the sanctification of the Name at its most extreme.' Marcel Dubois, 'Un regard chrétien sur l'Holocauste' (A Christian Looks at the Holocaust), in *Revue du service international de documentation judéo-chrétienne* vol. VII, no. 2 (1974) p. 11.

Henceforth 'he will see the light' (Isa. 53.11).[15] This is a promise of glorification for the whole of Israel, a guarantee of a final redemption in which the believer, illuminated by a grace of which he would be wrong to boast, can participate here and now in the secrecy of his faith.

What was accomplished in Christ in a single moment of time – a sort of transhistorical event – goes on happening through time in Israel. The Jewish people continues under our very eyes to carry the weight of history and to live out the night phase of the mystery of the Servant. Israel continues to experience the silence of God even though this silence does not discourage praying, profession of faith and affirmation of hope, all of them ongoing miracles, nor does this silence discourage Israel from scrutinizing its own history and that of the world at large for signs of the accomplishment of the promises. Its presence at our side obliges us to take seriously temporal reality[16] in all its incompleteness, just when we are settling all too readily into eternity. Israel makes us look at the sin of the world, our sin, and forbids us to overlook our own responsibility. By obliging us to take seriously that which in this world seems to belie Christian faith and its optimism, Israel gives us an opportune reminder that faith – because it is faith, that is to say anticipated participation in what flies in the face of the evidence – includes elements of silence, secrecy and incommunicability. The sheer absurdity of what Israel has borne[17] – absurdity beyond the power of language to express – makes it impossible to transform faith into ideology and disqualifies in advance pretentious claims at universal explanations. We are forbidden to forget that 'In hope, we already have salvation; in hope, not visibly present …' (Rom. 8.24).

[15] Jerusalem Bible translation, after the Greek and Qumran manuscripts.

[16] Cf. Abraham Heschel, *The Earth is the Lord's* (Woodstock, Vermont: Jewish Lights, 1995). Originally published by Farrar, Straus & Giroux, 1949.

[17] Cf. André Neher, *The Exile of the Word: From the Silence of the Bible to the Silence of Auschwitz* (translated from French by David Maisel; Philadelphia: Jewish Publication Society of America, 5741 [=1981]).

Evidence from Scripture

Such are the questions and the intuitions that recent history may bring to the Christian mind after centuries of anti-Judaism. Is it possible to meet them with any theological answers and arguments?

As we have seen, tradition offers us few usable elements enabling us to speak in positive terms of present-day Israel. Can we at the very least find within Scripture any guidelines to lead us in the direction of what we have been suggesting?

The first comment is obvious: on several occasions in the second part of the book of Isaiah, Israel is the one explicitly referred to as Servant (Isa. 41.8–9; 43.10; 44.1–2, 21; 45.4; 48.20; 49.3).[18] Unless we retreat into one variety or other of Marcionism, or stick to the theology of replacement in its most extreme form by affirming that the people of the Covenant has purely and simply ceased to exist outside the Church,[19] I cannot see for what reason or by what right Israel can be denied a title linked so intimately to its identity and mission. Its right to the title is indeed solemnly confirmed at the threshold of the New Testament (Luke 1.54).

The objection will undoubtedly be made that the coming of Christ and the proclamation of the gospel put the Jewish people into a 'profoundly different'[20] situation from that before Jesus Christ.

But is there any reason not to think that the present situation of Israel fits in precisely with the vocation of Servant as

---

[18] The fact that the identification is not explicit in Isa. 53 has not prevented Jewish tradition from applying this passage to Israel, even though apparently designating an individual rather than a collective. The objection is even less substantial once it is agreed that the fate of Israel is included within that of Jesus.

[19] Under one form or another, all these opinions are widespread throughout the Church today, whether implicitly or explicitly. But their theological basis is hardly strong enough for a contrary opinion to be judged heretical or even rash ...

[20] Cf. *infra*, n. 27.

described in ch. 53 of Isaiah? The subject will be discussed later: what St Paul calls the 'rejection' (Rom. 11.15) of Israel inevitably evokes the rejection of Christ in his passion and death as he took upon himself the fate of humankind cut off from God. If Christian tradition has claimed to point to the infidelity of Jews as the sole cause of the present situation of Israel, must we not also shed light on this situation by relating it to that of Christ, 'who became sin for us, so that in him we might become the righteousness of God' (2 Cor. 5.21)?

The connection is not unwarranted. It seems indeed to be supported by clear indications in the New Testament.

Although references to the Jews are scattered throughout the New Testament, we will refer once more to Romans ch. 11, and more precisely to the second part.

From the beginning of ch. 9 until ch. 11 v. 10, Paul seems uniquely preoccupied with the issue of the salvation of Jews who have not accepted the gospel: 'I could pray that I myself might be accursed and cut off from Christ, if this could benefit the brothers who are my own flesh and blood' (Rom. 9.3); 'my dearest wish and my prayer to God is [for the Israelites] that they might be saved' (Rom. 10.1). The question is that of the relation between the attitude of Jews toward the gospel and their own salvation. In this context, salvation of 'the Gentiles' is mentioned purely by way of contrast. The Gentiles have obtained righteousness by faith; Israel *did not succeed in fulfilling the Law* (cf. Rom. 9.31). In this context there is no relation between the 'lack of faith' of the Jews and the salvation of the Gentiles.

However, in v. 11 there is an abrupt change of perspective. From then onward, Paul establishes a direct relationship between the 'fault' or 'rejection'[21] of the Jews and the salvation

---

[21] To invoke the standing of the Jews in relation to the gospel and to qualify the situation henceforth to be theirs, Rom. 11 uses no less than 11 different terms translated by the New Jerusalem Bible as 'hardened', 'stumbling', 'downfall', 'fall', 'loss', 'rejection', 'branches cut off', 'unbelief', 'enemies', 'loved', 'disobedience'.

of the Gentiles: 'their failure has brought salvation for the Gentiles, in order to stir them to envy. And if their fall has proved a great gain to the world, and their loss has proved a great gain to the Gentiles – how much greater a gain will come when all is restored to them!' (Rom. 11.11–12). 'Since their rejection meant the reconciliation of the world, do you know what their re-acceptance will mean? Nothing less than life from the dead!' (Rom. 11.15). 'As regards the gospel, they are enemies, but for your sake' (Rom. 11.28). 'You have been shown mercy through their disobedience' (Rom. 11.30).

It goes without saying that a rather bland lesson can be drawn from these texts: every cloud has a silver lining; it was the Jewish refusal of the gospel that obliged the Apostles to turn to the Gentiles. However, such a reading does not appear to do justice to all that is contained within the texts. Because from v. 11 onward, we are in the presence of a situation in which the responsibility of the Jews, even though it continues to be affirmed, passes into the background and dwindles before the divine initiative. Such an initiative is suggested quite clearly by such terms as 'rejection' (Rom. 11.15) and especially 'hardening' (Rom. 11.7, 25). In the present situation of the Jews there is something largely beyond human responsibility: we are in the presence of a 'mystery' (Rom. 11.25), the evocation of which leads to the very mystery of God (Rom. 11.33–6). We are far from a simple set of circumstances favouring the spread of the gospel. There is a direct relationship not only between the 'lack of faith' of the Jews and the faith of the Gentiles but also between the 'rejection' or the humiliation of Israel – expressions that evoke the state of humiliation of the Servant at least as much as formal guilt – and the reconciliation of the world.

The word 'reconciliation' finally leads us to the most suggestive and indeed decisive argument of all.

In Rom. 5.10 Paul writes: 'For if, while we were enemies, we were reconciled to God through the death of his Son, how much more can we be sure that, being now reconciled, we shall be saved through his life!'

It is hard to avoid seeing a connection, both in structure and content between this verse on the one hand and verses 12 and 15 of ch. 11:

> 5.10 For if ... we were reconciled to God through the death of his Son,
> how much more, being now reconciled, we shall be saved through his life!
>
> 11.12 And if their fall has proved a great gain to the world, and their loss has proved a great gain to the Gentiles, how much greater a gain will come when all is restored to them!
>
> 11.15 Since their rejection meant the reconciliation of the world,
> do you know what their re-acceptance will mean? Nothing less than life from the dead!

The contexts are different but the connection is self-evident: there is a direct relationship between a fall and the salvation of the many. This is an argument *a fortiori*: the perspective of the raising up of what had been brought down, a raising up which is to bring about the fullness of salvation for the many. The parallel is even clearer when we notice that the 'reconciled' of 5.10 corresponds very closely to the 'reconciliation' of 11.15[22] and if we accept that 'life from the dead' (literally: 'life from among the dead') of 11.15 refers not only to the final destiny of Israel – already designated by the term 'acceptance'[23] – but also to that of the whole of humanity, according to the most probable exegesis. There are strong suggestions of a connection between the rejection of Israel and the death of Christ, and a connection between the acceptance of Israel and the resurrection of Christ.

---

[22] 'Reconcile' is the translation of *katallassó* and 'reconciliation' *katallagè*. With a single exception (1 Cor. 7.11) these terms, not common in the New Testament, designate reconciliation with God and accorded by God himself (cf. Rom. 5.11 and 2 Cor. 5.18, 21).

[23] 'Acceptance' is a translation of *prolempsis* which is a well-known hapax of the New Testament.

Likewise, there is a self-evident connection between the salvific aspect of the rejection – acceptance of Israel – and the salvific aspect of the death – resurrection of Christ. Unless one is willing to consider the possibility that the world has been reconciled twice, a close relationship between the rejection and subsequent acceptance of Israel on the one hand and the paschal mystery of Christ on the other can hardly be denied.

The abasement of the Servant (death of Christ, rejection of Israel) has already reconciled the world. His raising up is an even stronger cause of salvation. A raising up that has already been accomplished by the resurrection of Christ, but barely glimpsed in the case of Israel, for whom the second term, that of the raising up, is evoked in the form of questions referring to the future: 'how much greater a gain will come when all is restored to them!', 'do you know what their re-acceptance will mean? Nothing less than life from the dead!' The resurrected Christ gives us access in the hiddenness of faith to his final victory. The people of Israel, immersed within its ever-continuing history, continues to bear the weight of the sin of the world while it awaits its ultimate raising up which will be that of humanity itself.

A Proposal for a Synthesis

Before bringing together all the elements in a summary of the hypothesis, we need to foresee the misunderstandings that might be caused by describing the present-day situation of the Jewish people in a 'positive' light. It is important, therefore, to affirm that the situation of today's Jews is multifaceted with regard to Christian faith.

Like all people, Jews are sinners and do not escape from the universal need for redemption. In this respect there is no superiority of the Jew over the Greek.

The Jewish people as a whole has not recognized Jesus as Messiah or Son of God. The Christian, according to the New Testament, sees typical and symbolic significance in this refusal and in the situation that ensues from it. However, the Christian must avoid self-contradiction by forgetting or by pretending to forget that faith is a free gift which comes without any merit on his part and that guilt cannot therefore necessarily be attached to lack of faith.

Furthermore, the lack of recognition of Jesus by the Jewish people is ambivalent in itself: incorporated within the refusal of the idea of incarnation there is a positive affirmation of the transcendence and of the unity of God; in the refusal to acknowledge Jesus as Messiah is expressed the incomplete nature – the 'not yet' – of redemption: 'Yet at present we do not see everything subject to him' (Heb. 2.8).

Finally St Paul warns us that in the present situation of Israel there exists something beyond the responsibility of the Jews and which is a part of God's deliberate plans. We cannot therefore be allowed to overlook the fact that Scripture itself grants salvific meaning to what is called the 'hardening' of the Jews.

If such is the case, we must acknowledge that the people of Israel, in its present situation as well as throughout the centuries of history, in its suffering, hope and prayers has held to the mission of Servant.

This destiny is inseparable from that of the Gentiles. Israel bears the weight of the evil at work in the world, and its raising up will be that of humanity.

Nor is this destiny separable from that of the paschal mystery of Christ, which sheds light on it and fulfils it. This conclusion – an intuition of faith – is no more communicable than faith in Christ itself, and it must be lived out largely in silence; but it forbids the Christian to reduce the suffering of Israel to a matter of the punishment of the Jews.

By his resurrection, Christ gives us a pledge that Israel and the world will be raised up. By its endurance and by its hope, Israel reminds us of the historic and therefore unfinished character of redemption. While Christ gives us the assurance that redemption is 'already' here, Israel brings us back to the evidence for 'not yet'.

Finally, because the suffering endured by the Jewish people is in large measure due to Christians, its presence at our side under the appearance of the humiliated Servant forbids us to be arrogant (Rom. 11.18) and to forget our own need for redemption.

Is there any need to try to demonstrate the interest that the acknowledgement of Israel as Servant may have for theology?

We should first notice that, if true, such an acknowledgement must be made for itself quite independently of its potential usefulness. We cannot grasp the perspectives it opens up and the consequences it entails until we have recognized and accepted it.

Having said that, it may already be affirmed that recognition of Israel as Servant provides a foundation and an opening for theological reflection and for dialogue with Judaism. We make use of a term already full of biblical and theological substance. In so doing, we account for the permanence of Israel in its identity and election and at the same time we integrate what St Paul calls its 'rejection' without contradicting ourselves. We acknowledge that the present-day existence of the Jewish people is of significance and of salvific meaning in God's plans. We remain faithful to Christian faith, Christological and Christocentric, without refusing for all that to take into account the way the Jewish people perceives its own destiny in the light of its own tradition. We allow the Church of the Gentiles to situate herself in truthfulness in relation to Israel.

None of this can happen on the Christian side without true conversion. For we are required to situate ourselves in relation to Israel, and not just to situate Israel in relation to ourselves. This requires an experience of decentring and humility which is no threat to Christian faith but which does risk wounding centuries-old habits of self-sufficiency. For 'Christiano-centrism' if one may dare to use such an expression, constantly threatens to take the place of true Christo-centrism in Christian thinking. And if the Church proclaims that all people are 'ordained' to belong to the messianic people inaugurated in Jesus Christ,[24] she cannot, for all that, forget

---

[24] Dogmatic Constitution *Lumen Gentium*, 16.

that she herself can understand her own mystery only with reference to Israel (Eph. 2.1–3, 6) who, even when 'rejected', always precedes her in election and to whom she owes her grafting into the Covenant (cf. Rom. 11.19).[25]

Questions

There remain a certain number of questions, none of which can be answered in a few lines but which are nevertheless unavoidable. Here we will mention three of the main ones.[26]

The first concerns, of course, the identity of the Jewish people at the present time. Can Christian faith truly admit, while remaining self-consistent, that the people of the First Covenant can persist 'in the time of the Gentiles?' According to the declaration of the Roman Commission for Religious Relations with the Jews, 'the history of Judaism did not end with the destruction of Jerusalem, but rather went on to develop a religious tradition. Although we believe that the importance of that tradition has acquired a profoundly different meaning with the coming of Christ, it is nonetheless rich in religious values'.[27] Is this phrase to be understood in a restrictive manner so as to deduce from it that, for the Church, Judaism is no more than a religious tradition bearing 'values'? Are we permitted to think that even when placed in a 'profoundly different' situation, it remains the chosen people, the destiny of which is of concern to humanity? In the Constitution on the Church, Vatican II designates it as 'this People'.[28]

The second question has to do with the value and authority

---

[25] Cf. *Nostra Aetate* no. 4.

[26] In addition to the question of the authority of Christian tradition on the point. Cf. *supra*, n. 9.

[27] Cf. *Nostra Aetate* no. 4; Guidelines and Suggestions for implementing the Conciliar Declaration *Nostra Aetate* no. 4, by the Vatican Commission for Religious Relations with the Jews, 19 January 1975. In Croner (ed.) *Stepping Stones to further Jewish–Christian Relations*, p. 11.

[28] *Lumen Gentium*, 16.

that Christianity can acknowledge as due to Jewish spiritual and theological tradition after Jesus Christ. Can Christian thought take into account the manner in which contemporary Judaism continues to search the Scriptures?[29] Or as it is occasionally said, could the Holy Spirit have deserted Israel so that all readings of Scripture that are not explicitly Christological risk, from that very fact, being aberrant and therefore without meaning? At bottom this question is an extension of the former: what is at issue here is to know whether the Church and Judaism are purely and simply external to each other. There has undoubtedly been a break between the two, which have become de facto external to each other ever since Christians were expelled from the synagogue in the first century and since the Judaeo-Christian movement in the Church became extinct in practical terms three centuries later. But this de facto situation which was a literal tearing apart in the first case and an anomaly in the second – for by its very nature the Church draws its origins from Israel and from the Gentiles[30] – does not answer the question: are the Church and Judaism in their very essence external to each other? Short of holding that the entire heritage of the Covenant has been transferred to the Church, in which case Judaism represents no more than a survival of a religious tradition, we cannot avoid the question as to how Israel and the Church, both of which exist only in and by this unique Covenant,[31] are related to each other within it.

[29] '... The real issue is not so much appreciation of the Jewish phenomenon in the light of Christian revelation, indispensable though a turnabout may be on this level, as acknowledgement of present-day Jewish existence and conduct as theological necessity within the plan of God, and of its perfectioning with time'. Kurt Hruby, 'Les Relations entre le judaïsme et l'Eglise, Jalons de réflexion théologique' (Relations between Judaism and the Church: Markers of theological thought) in *Rencontre*, 63/4 (1979), 34, and *Sens*, 12 (1979) (joint number).

[30] Cf. Francesco Rossi de Gasperis, 'Israele o la radice santa della nostra fede', *Rassegna di Teologia* (1980), no. 1, pp. 1–15; no. 2, pp. 116–29.

[31] 'One of the major anomalies inherent in the new developments occurring within Christianity is that in virtually every field, theological, liturgical, institutional, the Christian faith appears to be radically "other" with

Finally, in respect of the meaning of Jewish existence after Christ, must we rely on a literal reading of Scripture, including the New Testament, to shed light on it? Or rather, must we use Scripture to attempt to understand a history that continues to develop before our eyes and which St Paul obviously could not know?

Tradition, as already mentioned, is of no great help in finding answers to these questions. But it would be a mistake to use this fact as an argument to ignore them if, as we may legitimately think, this silence of tradition is itself equivocal. Indeed, the silence can be attributed to motives quite other than respectfulness towards a 'mystery'. On this point we shall conclude.

We have already remarked that when Vatican II speaks of the Jews, it uses scriptural or theological language only for commenting on the origins of the Church and on eschatological perspectives. As far as the reciprocal situation of the Church and of the Jewish people at the present time is concerned, the Council limits itself to generalities on universal love. With respect to the sufferings of the Jewish people, the manner in which the hatreds, persecutions and all the displays of anti-Semitism directed against Jews at any time and from any source are 'deplored', may strike the observer as timid.[32]

Whereas the Council is careful to be very precise about Jewish responsibility for the death of Jesus – in order, let it be stressed, to set limits to this responsibility – the 'persecutions' of which the Jews have been the victims are contained within a

---

cont.
respect to Judaism to such a degree that continuity has become masked by too many different elements to be immediately and directly perceptible. In the course of its development, Christianity has become effectively "another religion" and its theological expression has always powerfully accentuated this aspect for fear of "judaisation". The fact that this sort of development more and more distanced the Christian community from its roots and from its original inspiration has gone unnoticed.' Kurt Hruby, 'Les Relations entre le judaïsme et l'Eglise', p. 33.

[32] *Nostra Aetate* no. 4.

double generalization. In the first place, the Church deplores them because she 'repudiates all persecutions against any man'.[33] It is within this general framework that the persecutions against the Jews are deplored 'because of the patrimony she shares with the Jews'.[34] Later, persecutions against the Jews are deplored 'from any source'.

In a nutshell, no mention is made of the specific character of the persecution of the Jews. While care is taken to be very precise about the specific responsibility of Jews for the death of Christ, nothing is said of any specific responsibility that Christians may bear for anti-Semitic persecutions.

In accepting that Jewish suffering – and the responsibility of Christians for the suffering of the Jews – is in a category apart, and in recognizing the destiny of the Servant in the sufferings of Israel, we acknowledge that the Servant bore *our* sufferings, endured *our* pains, was broken on account of *our* wickedness. We acknowledge that we have made common cause with the world in the death of the Servant and that we too are on the side of the Gentiles in the sufferings of Israel. Admittedly, the Church is not simply to be identified with the Gentiles or with 'the world' of sin. From her beginnings she has lived and continues to live with her Lord the condition of the persecuted Righteous one in visible or hidden communion with the mystery of Israel. But the affirmation that the Church is the body and bride of Christ cannot mask the other reality concerning the special responsibility of Christians for the sufferings endured by the Jewish people. In this respect the situation of Christians is no less ambivalent in its own way than that of the Jews. To study the horrendous history of anti-Semitism,[35] overwhelming for us, is to perceive that nowhere

[33] *Nostra Aetate* no. 4.

[34] *Nostra Aetate* no. 4.

[35] Bibliography in Leon Poliakov, *History of Anti-Semitism* (4 vols.; New York: Vanguard, 1976): vol. 3 (transl. George Klin): *From Voltaire to Wagner*. Cf. F. Lovsky, *L'antisémitisme chrétien* (*Christian Anti-Semitism*), in French (Paris: Cerf, 1970), pp. 377–80.

did the Jews suffer more than within the Christian world. No theology of history can spare itself from deep reflection on this fact.[36] The vocation of the Church is to bring about reconciliation of Israel and the Gentiles (cf. Eph. 3). In essence, this reconciliation has already been achieved – *already* given though *not yet* visibly accomplished – in Christ's Passover. But between the beginning and the eschatological accomplishment, during the unfolding of the history in which we find ourselves immersed, and in which vocation takes the form of a task to be accomplished, the Church should have been inspired, as she still should be, with a lasting determination to bring about reconciliation between Israel and the Gentiles. This determination should arise from her awareness of her own identity. Now, the very least that can be said is that the Church has not done all that has been in her power to make the Gentiles love Israel nor to make Israel love the Gentiles.

In the Shoah Israel experienced not only the silence of God but also the silence of the Gentiles. It is impossible to break this silence without admitting our guilt. In other words, the Church of the Gentiles cannot make a specific statement about Israel without situating herself in relation to Israel. Situating herself in relation to Israel carries the recognition that Israel is the one who bears our sin. Recognition cannot go without repentance.[37] 'For God has bound all men over to disobedience so that he may have mercy on them all' (Rom. 11.32).

✡ ✡ ✡

André Neher has asked whether 'philosophy is yet ready for an evaluation of Auschwitz as an example of universal human suffering'.[38] We must ask ourselves the same question about Christian theology.

---

[36] We might also wonder whether a theology of history could neglect taking into account the reality and meaning of Jewish existence without running the risk of losing its way in abstraction or ideology.

[37] On Christian repentance, see in particular Lovsky, *La déchirure de l'absence* (see *supra*, n. 2).

[38] Neher, *The Exile of the Word*, p. 141.

For centuries the Church reproached the Jews for their blindness with regard to Jesus. Using the verse of St Paul that refers to the veil covering the hearts of the Israelites (2 Cor. 3.15), she turned this veil into a blindfold which she placed on the eyes of the synagogue.

Perhaps one day the Gentiles themselves will open their eyes to recognize in Israel the features of the Servant. On that day 'they will look on the one they have pierced' (John 19.37; cf. Zech. 12.10).

PART 2

On the Shoah

A Reflection on the Genocide

Introduction

It is impossible to refer to the Jewish people today without mentioning in some way or other what is commonly referred to as the 'Holocaust' which, for reasons to be explained later, is preferably designated by the Hebrew term 'Shoah'.

Explicitly or implicitly and whether we like it or not, the Nazi genocide is present in our discourse on Judaism and in our encounters with the Jews. Anyone who might claim to disregard this reality is obliged to accept as obvious the following fact: it is during the past few decades that the Christian Churches have really started to undertake research in Judaism and in the significance of Jewish existence. Virtually all the great documents striving to break with a past of anti-Judaism or theological anti-Semitism and using fresh terms to reflect on Judaism after Jesus Christ have appeared since the Second World War.[1] This is a fact which in itself deserves to hold our attention and it demonstrates the extent to which it would be illusory to want to talk about Judaism while ignoring the attempt to exterminate the Jewish people in our own days at the very heart of the Christian world. Before Auschwitz, could Christian thinking have taken a fresh look at the significance of the permanence of Israel? No doubt, it is somewhat pointless to ask such a question but at the moment of embarking on such research, it would be equally pointless to pass over in silence the reasons that have made such questioning inevitable. At a time when the Churches are pondering a fresh approach to the question of the Jewish people, we are not entitled to excuse ourselves from reflecting on the event which has been the direct cause of the change in attitude.

---

[1] H. Croner (compiler) *Stepping Stones to further Jewish-Christian Relations* (London and New York: Stimulus Books, 1977); *More Stepping Stones* (New York: Paulist Press, 1985). M.-T. Hoch and B. Dupuy, *Les Églises devant le judaïsme. Documents officiels 1948–1978* (*The Churches in Face of Judaism*), in French. A collection of translated texts with commentary (Paris: Cerf, 1980).

3

Silence

However, the first things that come to mind as soon as we set out to think about the subject, are the reasons that ought to dissuade us from speaking about it. There is something derisory, indecent even, in the idea of talking about Auschwitz, all the more so when the talk is faith-based. There are all sorts of reasons for remaining silent. Before going any further, it is necessary to examine them. Not to try to refute them, but on the contrary, to sort out within what limits and under what conditions we may be allowed to speak.

Silence in the Face of Evil

The first reason has to do with the impossibility of speaking of suffering and evil in general. Ordinary experience attests to the fact that suffering is one of those realities that words cannot express.[1]

The book of Job seems even to suggest that there is a mysterious symmetry between God and evil and that this symmetry is displayed in the inability of human speech to express the one or the other. The only answer that Job gets in his bafflement over the enigma of his own suffering, is another question: 'What about God? Do you understand him?' This

---

[1] A few days before his death, Cardinal Veuillot confided to one of his close associates: 'We know how to say fine things about suffering. I myself have talked feelingly about it. Tell the priests to say nothing about it. We do not know what it is ...' (Documentation catholique no. 1512, 3 March 1968, col. 436).

saying explains nothing, neither evil nor God. We simply come to see that there exists an analogy between the futility of words about suffering and the futility of words about God. Theology, which does not delude itself about its ability to reason about God, has found it necessary to forge the term 'apophatism' to affirm that God must be spoken of in the negative mode: to say what God is not since we cannot say what God is. The experience and awareness of the derisory character of language in the face of reality, force the person attempting to speak of evil and suffering to keep a sort of distance that can also be qualified as apophatic. There exist realities too far beyond words for us to be able to speak about them without weakening them or misinterpreting them.

Without a doubt that is the cause of the unease we may feel when reading books on suffering that are written too stylishly. It is hard to avoid a certain kind of falseness when evil is turned into the object of a literary exercise. Words are necessary, but they have an unfortunate tendency to attract attention to themselves and insidiously to take the place of what they refer to, ultimately pushing into the background what they set out to demonstrate. So we have to show a corresponding vigilance against the danger of theological formulations which manage to hide the very thing they are meant to express. Discourse fails its purpose if it cannot allow silence to take over from language at the proper time.

Is a 'Theology' of Auschwitz Possible?

The second reason is inherent within the enterprise itself: is a *theological* discourse on the Shoah possible? There is no theology which is not rooted within a tradition, that is to say within the religious experience of a believing people. On what tradition can a 'theology' of Auschwitz be based? On this subject – and for good reason – there are no teachings of the Fathers or of the great theologians. In Christian teaching of the past thirty years, is it possible to find material for a reflection of this type? Has the manner of believing, speaking or praying of Christians been specially affected by the shock of the genocide? The enormous quantity of historical literature and journalistic writing that has accumulated is in marked contrast to the restricted amount of Christian reflection on the issue of the Final Solution. 'The death of God' has been written about but, with few exceptions, Christian thought has not given the genocide anything like the attention that the subject deserves. Do we have to trace this reserve to a kind of stupor engendered by a reality that reduces language to impotence, or, on the contrary, by an inability to grasp the irreducible singularity of Auschwitz?

Nor can Christian memory find any experience or significant precedent in our history that could be used to formulate a theological discourse today. Jewish tradition can refer back to events, the importance and especially the significance of which are comparable to that of the Shoah: the Exile and the two destructions of the Temple, but even in the Jewish mind the genocide may perhaps involve something that renders it qualitatively different from the earlier catastrophes. What is certain is that nothing in Christian tradition can be compared to these events. The attempt to exterminate generations of martyrs gives us little help in that it was part of an experience that, unlike the Shoah, took place inside the Church. It is truly tragic that the Shoah, insofar as it happened outside the boundaries of the Church, has remained *ipso facto* outside the boundaries of our reflection. And no one, it is to be hoped, would dare to apply to the genocide the interpretation that the generation of the Fathers thought they could give of the destruction of Jerusalem by the armies of Titus, seeing therein the operation of divine justice. If any judgement was at work in the Shoah, we have good reason to think that the verdict falls on the Gentiles rather than on Israel.

We are therefore confronted with a dilemma. Should we speak of the Shoah in terms of generalities about evil, sin, suffering and death, giving each of these notions a quantitative coefficient or superlative as may be needed? In such a case, in the last analysis the Shoah is ultimately reduced to another example of something familiar and the attempt to wipe out the Jewish people is deprived of the very particular significance it may have from the point of view of Christian faith. The alternative is to try to grasp and express this specific element in all its singularity and to affirm at the same time that in our time an event has taken place whose complete newness obliges us to construct a completely new discourse.

How then are we to tackle the 'apartness' of this event when there is no tradition to lean on, without falling into the trap of playing the part of prophets or wandering off into illuminism? Here we find ourselves confronted with a reality from which it is not open to us to avert our gaze (see Isa. 53.3), even though we cannot decipher its meaning.

There is, therefore, a great temptation to make a bypass around the question posed to faith and to express ourselves merely in terms of human rights, of racism and of persecution. This was the option followed by the Second Vatican Council (for reasons which this is not the place to judge) in a text of incontestable quality and beauty. In the five lines in which the Council 'deplores' the long tragedy of anti-Semitic persecutions, no explicit mention is made, however, of the Shoah. This silence is all the more remarkable in that, without the events directly linked to Nazism, the Council would have been unlikely to have included a reflection on Judaism in its programme of work.[2]

We have mentioned that for Christianity there is no precedent in terms of a model that might help us to look at the Shoah from the point of view of faith. But in fact the link between the sufferings of the Jewish people and those of the Lord's Servant evoked in Isaiah ch. 53 is so strong, that the Christian is compellingly led to search within Holy Scripture for the enlightenment needed. There, we find that the only true precedent capable of guiding our reflection on the passion of

---

[2] Cf. René Laurentin, *L'Eglise et les juifs à Vatican II* (*The Church and the Jews at Vatican II*), in French (Tournai: Casterman, 1967), pp. 11–12.

Israel is the passion and death of Jesus of Nazareth, events in which Christian faith sees the realization of the words of the prophet. But dare we claim that in our days there has been an event linked in such a special way to the death of Jesus? This is no minor question for Christian faith. Do our awareness of the many implications involved and our lack of tools to enable us to formulate an answer further constrain us to remain silent?

Has the Church the Right to Speak?

There is another argument for remaining silent, and it is put to us by voices both within and without the Christian world; it is said that the Church has lost the right to speak. For the past seventeen centuries has she not compromised herself by too many historical errors to have the right to raise her voice? Particularly in relation to the sufferings of Israel, does not the Church carry a heavy load of responsibility for the conditions endured by the Jews down the centuries, for the arguments she provided to anti-Semitism, for the abuse of her own power or, on the contrary, for her silence and her omissions? Whatever the attitudes, the devotion and even the heroism that came from the Christian world during the Nazi period, how can it be denied that the Shoah was the culmination of a historical process in which the Church – as I will have occasion to repeat – was far from innocent? Do not these facts disqualify her irremediably? How can she, a few short years after the event, claim to be able to throw light on it in the language of an abstract and wholly illusory neutrality?

Repentance or Bad Conscience?

And if she does speak in a mood of repentance, as more and more Christians are pressing her to do, would such a move not look like an attempt to rid herself of guilt? The new interest shown by a growing number of Christians in all things Jewish is in fact interpreted in this way by some, and not only by Jews.

'Holocaust'?

Such are the principal reasons that might discourage any desire to apply any kind of language of faith to the recent sufferings of the Jewish people.

It is my reluctance to accept easy explanations for something by nature absurd that deters me from using the massively popular term 'Holocaust' for the Final Solution. There are two reasons why this term seems inappropriate.

In the biblical tradition, the term 'holocaust' designates a sacrifice in which the victim is totally destroyed by fire. With reference to the death camps, the comparison is shocking and inadmissible. Above all, it should be remembered that genocide is not in itself a sacrifice: the members of the SS were not *cohanim*,[3] their aim was not to render glory to God and we would never dream of supposing that God himself could have wanted or taken pleasure in their deeds. It is true that certain victims who are known to God freely offered up their lives in the Shoah and died 'sanctifying the Name'. Here, the Christian cannot avoid thinking of the manner in which Jesus by a free-will act transformed into a spiritual sacrifice a death that was hardly a liturgical ceremony either in itself or in the intention of those who carried it out. The habitual use of the term 'sacrifice' to describe the death of Jesus – or of martyrs – should not blind us to the fact that it is justified only at the cost of a reinterpretation through faith. Nothing authorizes us to give the Shoah, as such, a similar interpretation. Besides, a large number of victims did not experience it as a holocaust, but as a tragic absurdity.

To stamp the genocide with the holocaust label gives it some kind of meaning. However, no label, no definition can ever give

---

[3] Jewish priests who offered sacrifices in the Temple.

a satisfactory meaning to an event characterized first and foremost by its meaninglessness. But here we must recognize that an unbalanced way of speaking of the resurrection all too often prevents Christians from reflecting on the reality of evil itself.

Let us add that the giving of a meaning, and moreover a religious meaning, brings about an attenuation of the scandal by suggesting some form of legitimization. This is also the inherent risk of applying such terms as 'vocation' or 'destiny' to Jewish existence. Such words – which cannot be totally avoided – carry the danger of appearing to justify what is unjustifiable. We must repeat: if there is anything to be found in the Shoah beyond meaninglessness, it can be found only in the way in which the victims were able to offer up freely their own lives. But there is no way – and for good reason – in which such a meaning can be applied from outside.

For all these reasons, the Hebrew word 'Shoah' is to be preferred to 'holocaust'. Within the Jewish world 'Shoah' is the term generally used to designate Hitler's genocide. It can be rendered in English by 'catastrophe' or even better, 'cataclysm'. The term limits itself to designate the event in all its unpredictable and incomprehensible brutality without claiming to suggest any possible significance. We may add that the term can also evoke primitive chaos, and that certain authors have asked whether Auschwitz should not be considered as the beginning of a new era.[4]

✡ ✡ ✡

I have stated some reasons for remaining silent. If I now start considering arguments in favour of speaking out, I would not want it to be suggested that these latter are overwhelmingly stronger than the former. The questions and objections I have brought forward must be kept in mind. To a large extent they remain unresolved. They mark out limits and call for a certain

---

[4] Eva Fleischner (ed.), *Auschwitz, Beginning of a New Era? Reflexions on the Holocaust* (New York: KTAV, 1977).

particular type of language. And if eventually the decision is made to break the silence in order to say that which must be said, it will always be on a foundation of silence. It is only on this condition that speech may be licit.

Unveiling

If, after having given birth to Christianity, the Jewish people had disappeared from history as did the Etruscans or the Toltecs, how would our manuals of theology have had to be changed or cut? Are there, for instance, treatises on the Church that take into consideration the existence of an Israel contemporary to Christianity, other than in the form of an appendix or an annexe, and which do not dodge the question this permanence represents for Christian faith? For its part, the Constitution on the Church of Vatican II mentions the Jewish people only to put them in the first rank of those who have not yet received the gospel, while introducing a strange and inexplicable qualification into an unequivocal affirmation of the Epistle to the Romans.[1] According to *Lumen Gentium*, the difference between the Jews and other non-Christians is apparently only in the distance that separates them both from the gospel. And if history shows that the paths of Jews and Christians 'constantly criss-cross',[2] theology on its part, has shown itself to be 'extremely simplistic', in the words of F. Lovsky,[3] concerning the permanence of Judaism.

To quote the same author, it may be asked whether it is routine alone which explains the lack of attention that until

---

[1] Constitution *Lumen Gentium*, no. 16. Where Rom. 9.4, quoted in part by the conciliar text, makes use of an elliptical phrase ('those to whom ... the covenants') usually translated in the present tense (NIV: 'Theirs is...'), the Council introduces the words *data fuerunt* ('to whom the testament and the promises *were given*').

[2] Statement by the French Bishops' Committee for Relations with Jews, April 1973. Translated from French. In Croner (ed.), *Stepping Stones*, p. 60.

[3] Lovsky, *La déchirure de l'absence*, p. 39.

recently Christian thinking has directed to the Jewish people. Experience has shown that the simple fact of speaking of the Jews in non-hostile terms can incur the accusation of 'putting the Christian faith in danger'. In this respect some of the opinions expressed in the francophone world in opposition to the 'Pastoral orientations' published in April 1973 by the French Episcopal Committee for Relations with Judaism were particularly significant. The concern to defend orthodoxy, affirmed explicitly in some of these reactions, seems all the more unexpected, in that it comes from theologians who are not in the habit of taking themselves for new Torquemadas.[4]

The fact is that Christian thinking has purely and simply repressed those questions with which the permanence of Judaism confronts it. And if God, in the expression of Maurice Clavel, is the great repressed in the modern mind, it is easy to see that Israel is, or has been the great repressed in the Christian mind. Israel's refusal to disappear has caught out a theology that had found no place for Judaism in its syntheses except in assigning it a negative role, thus implying an image of it pretty distant from reality. It may even be asked whether the caricature, crude or subtle, constantly given of the Jew in Christian teaching, did not proceed from a need for defence against the questions which would inevitably have followed the discovery of what Israel really is. Simply by their existence, the Jewish people act as an irritant in the physical sense of the word.

F. Lovsky remarks that 'the old theory of rejection broods over the rejection of Israel with vindictive delight as if it were preparing the indictment for a celestial prosecutor. The modern theology of the rejection scornfully denies the originality of the people of Israel in order to dissolve it in the sundry collection of peoples of the 19th and 20th centuries'.[5] There can be no doubt that the refusal to recognize any originality in whatever is Jewish finds a special application in the refusal to recognize that the genocide has any unique character. Concerning the Shoah

---

[4] See for instance reactions published in *Témoignage chrétien*, 26 April 1973.
[5] Lovsky, *La déchirure de l'absence*, p. 39.

there is a suspicious silence which comes from the refusal to hear certain questions or to face certain facts. Here, the reasons listed above for keeping silent can provide a dubious legitimacy for the haste of those who want us to turn the page to catch up with the progress of a history that has seen a good many other crimes since those of Hitler. There are even Christians who show astonishment at Jews brooding over grievances thirty years old which they seem so incapable of forgetting [6] to the point where the observation becomes an apologetic argument, with a contrast drawn between the incapacity of Jews to shed their past and the Christian readiness to forgive. This is a special application of a relatively classic attitude on the part of Christians which consists of taking oneself for that which one wishes to be, while laying on the Jew the obligation to practise the ideal of the gospel. This attitude is particularly out of place here, and it also displays a dismaying inability to grasp what this thing is about.

The simple fact that attempts are made to repress the questions raised by the destiny of the Jews is enough to indicate that such questions are in fact absolutely crucial.

The Shoah is a vehicle of revelation: it brings out realities we are obliged to confront.

Evil

The Shoah is an open demonstration of the evil present in this world.

In a text entitled 'What the Holocaust Was Not', Emil Fackenheim rules out one by one all the general headings under which the Shoah might be included. He writes that the Holocaust was not a war: the Jews did not have any power and the danger they posed to the security of the Reich existed only in the imagination of the Nazis. Neither was it a war crime:

---

[6] Cf. J.-M. Paupert, 'Letter to my Jewish friends', in *Le Monde*, 4–5 January 1981, pp. 1 and 6.

even if perpetrated during the war, the genocide was not linked to the pursuit of any military objective or to the course of the hostilities. Neither was it a racist act: the simple fact that the title of 'Honorary Aryans' was given to the Japanese is enough to show that if the Nazis were racist, it was only insofar as they were anti-Semitic and not vice versa. And even, paradoxically, Fackenheim goes so far as to maintain that the Holocaust was not a genocide: there is no doubt, he writes, that the term was invented as a designation of Hitler's attempt to destroy the Jewish people. But the word, unfortunately, has found so many other uses since then that it has come to designate other things than those evoked the first time it was used; today the term even risks masking its essential character. Modern genocides are always provoked by motives explicable in human terms: greed, hatred, xenophobia, even when these motives are masked by ideologies. In Hitler's genocide, the ideology expressed had one openly admitted aim: to rid the world of Jews as one rids oneself of vermin.[7]

In this way genocide demonstrates a free and absolute will to destroy human beings. This has been shown over and over again by witnesses to the Final Solution and its methods: the objective, even above the physical liquidation of victims, was their dehumanization. Here, evil shows itself in its purest form, freed from all the motivations or justifications to which the crime is usually linked: economic, political, military, emotional or any other. One finds oneself facing an urge to kill apparently sufficient in itself and acting as its own justification. And that, not because of some private perversity, but on a scale in which humanity finds itself implicated, directly or not. In the Shoah the evil present in the heart of humankind takes shape and shows itself in broad daylight. The human sciences can be left to untangle causes and meanings. But the believer, for his part, cannot avoid two inescapable facts: the first is the reality of evil in this world; Scripture tells us that 'the whole world is under

---

[7] Emil L. Fackenheim, 'What the Holocaust Was Not', in *Face to Face, An interreligious bulletin*, 7 (winter 1980), pp. 8–9, Anti-defamation league of B'nai B'rith, New York.

the control of the evil one' (1 John 5.19). The second is that the evil that plagues humanity was focused for one moment in time on the people chosen to be the sign of the presence of God in this world.

The Sin of Christians

In revealing the sin of the world, the Shoah highlights in a special way the particular sin of Christians.

Having said that, we must guard ourselves against being simplistic and adding yet more grievances to an already overloaded charge sheet. The Church does indeed bear a heavy responsibility for the very existence of the conditions that made the genocide possible. But it would go against historical truth to claim that the Final Solution was adopted in a strict continuity from the anti-Semitism of the Fathers of the Church and of Christendom, to the extent of constituting its logical and obligatory culmination. There is no need to remind ourselves that Nazi paganism also attacked Christian communities; many are the members of the different Churches who paid with their lives for the prophetic courage with which they opposed its pretensions. For its part, Christian anti-Semitism has never aimed at the physical suppression of the Jewish people. St John Chrysostom and St Augustine never desired the disappearance of a people whose fall, according to their theology, gave providential witness to divine justice and whose permanence was essential to support the faith and fear of God in believers coming from paganism. There is no doubt that the ancient reserve of anti-Semitism inherited from pagan antiquity and reinforced by theological arguments from the polemic with the synagogue has led Christians throughout the centuries to acts of bloody violence against the persons of Jews.[8] But the Church, whose Scriptures tell her that Israel has been 'hardened' until its

---

[8] Generally against the wishes of Bishops and other ecclesiastics who tried to protect Jews against popular violence.

final conversion, has never wished for nor encouraged in any
way the disappearance of Israel.[9]

Let us remember that the idea of race, in the modern sense of
this term, has never been part of the Christian conception of
Jewishness and that, in principle, a baptized Jew has never been
subjected to discrimination because of his origin.

There are, therefore, too many differences between Christian
anti-Semitism and Nazi racism to enable the establishment of
any real continuity between the two. Aryan ideology has its
own roots that are not to be found within Christian tradition.

Having said that, it would go against the evidence not to
recognize that some responsibility weighs upon the Church for
the long-term preparation of a climate in which genocide was
possible. There is no way of knowing how St John Chrysostom
would have behaved had he been bishop in Nazi Germany. It
may be supposed that the pastoral lucidity which led him to the
self-imposed duty of using invective and boorishness against
Jews would have shown him where the real danger lay; he
might have spoken of Jews in terms other than those he used
when trying to dissuade the Christians of Antioch from going
to the synagogue.[10] Without a doubt Chrysostom represents an
extreme case but he is unique only insofar as he constitutes a

---

[9] Y. Congar, 'Le peuple de Dieu dans l'Eglise ancienne'. (The People of
God in the Ancient Church) in *Rencontre*, 6th year (1972), nos. 25–6, pp. 51–
2. According to D. Judant, the idea of a general conversion of the Jewish
people at the end of time did not form a part of the thinking of the Fathers in
general and became accepted only after the patristic era, 'even though it has
neither scriptural nor theological basis and does not correspond to the
apostolic tradition'. D. Judant; *Judaïsme et Christianisme. Dossier patristique*
(Paris: Cèdre, 1969) pp. 258 and 260. Marcel Simon's opinion on this subject
is more qualified (Simon, *Verus Israel*, p. 119 and n. 2).

[10] 'The temple was already a den of thieves when the Jewish
commonwealth and way of life still prevailed. Now you give it a name more
worthy than it deserves if you call it a brothel, a stronghold of sin, a lodging-
place for demons, a fortress of the devil, the destruction of the soul, the
precipice and pit of all perdition, or whatever name you give it.' Discourse VI
in *Saint John Chrysostom: Discourses against Judaizing Christians* (transl. by Paul
W. Harkins; Washington, DC: Catholic University of America Press, 1979),
p. 174.

peak. Our tradition, whether liturgical, artistic, catechetical or theological, is strongly marked by a style of teaching which could go as far as making hatred of the Jew a duty of conscience and which at best (with rare exceptions) lacked warmth. What was sown throughout the history of the Church was fatally bound to bear fruit. The Christian people had too little love for Jews to be able to act effectively in their support when needed.[11] The Church was in no position to check a flood of hatred which she had helped to prepare – even if involuntarily – over a long period of time. There appears to have been a great lack of spiritual sensitivity as well as of historical perceptiveness. Despite the warning of Pius XI ('Spiritually, we are all Semites'), did Christians feel pain in their own flesh because of the wounds of the Jews? Anti-Semitism, that blemish on the history of the Christian world, reached a tragic culmination in the Shoah.

There is no point in trying to evaluate or quantify the part due to Christianity in the misfortunes that fell on the Jewish people.

[11] On 7 August 1941 Marshal Pétain asked his ambassador at the Holy See, Léon Bérard, to let him know the opinion of the Vatican on the legislation of the French State concerning Jews. In his answer, dated 2 September 1941, L. Bérard wrote: 'I can affirm that it does not appear that the pontifical authority is either occupied or preoccupied with this part of French politics and that until now no complaint or request coming from France has given it an opportunity of this kind ... In principle, there is nothing in these measures [the law of 2 June 1941 on the status of Jews] that can be a cause for criticism, from the point of view of the Holy See which considers that in passing such measures a State is making legitimate use of its power and that there is no place for spiritual power to insinuate itself within the interior policy of States. Besides, the Church has never professed that the same rights must be accorded or granted to every citizen. She has never ceased to teach the dignity and respect of the human person. But one can be sure that she does not take the same view of these things, or in so rigorous a manner as the spiritual heirs of Rousseau or Condorcet ... I learnt from official sources at the Vatican that no action will be taken against us concerning the status of the Jews ...' The full text of L. Bérard's report is to be found in J. Nobecourt, *Le 'Vicaire' et l'histoire* (Paris: Seuil, 1964), pp. 356–62. Cf. M.-R. Marrus and R. O. Paxton, *Vichy France and the Jews* (New York: Basic Books, 1981).

Without claiming to retrace the history of anti-Semitism or to analyse it here, we must nevertheless record that, in Christian hostility toward Jews, there enters an original element which cannot be reduced to the ancient pagan anti-Semitism which survived the teaching of the gospel. To the eternal accusations against the Jews, repeated under varying forms ever since Antiquity, Christianity did in fact add its own themes and arguments. According to Marcel Simon 'Christian anti-Semitism is above all an expression of the disappointment brought about by the resistance of Israel'.[12] Directly linked to the refusal with which Jews oppose Christian preaching, this so-called spiritual attitude takes from Revelation itself its grievances and its weapons. The preaching of the Prophets has supplied an inexhaustible repertory of polemic against the synagogue; it has appeared to lend support to the hostility or the conceit which converted pagans constantly nurtured towards the Israelites. Jews were impious, grasping, debauched; this was attested to by Scripture and the prophets had made such accusations over and over again ... When pronounced within Israel, the prophetic word is a call to conversion. When the same word is repeated outside and turned against the Jews, it becomes a justification for a transfer of responsibility: it is the Jews who are the sinners because Scripture says so. Their rejection of Christ, setting the seal on their sinfulness, makes them living symbols of closedness to grace.[13] Thus Revelation

---

[12] Simon, *Verus Israel*, p. 245.

[13] 'But what is the source of this hardness? It comes from gluttony and drunkenness. Who says so? Moses himself. "Israel ate and was filled and the darling grew fat and frisky" (Deut. 32.15). When brute animals feed from a full manger, they grow plump and become more obstinate and hard to hold in check; they endure neither the yoke, the reins, nor the hand of the charioteer. Just so the Jewish people were driven by their drunkenness and plumpness to the ultimate evil; they kicked about, they failed to accept the yoke of Christ, nor did they pull the plow of his teaching. Another prophet hinted at this when he said: "Israel is as obstinate as a stubborn heifer". And still another called the Jews "an untamed calf".' Discourse I, in Harkins (trans.), *Saint John Chrysostom, op. cit.* p. 8.

supports pagan arrogance, or, if the term is given the meaning it has acquired in Christian tradition, its pharisaism. The prophetic word was pronounced as a call to repentance but it became an encouragement to search out sinfulness in the consciences of others.

In its principle and in the mechanisms it brings into play, Christian anti-Semitism expresses as clearly as possible the refusal of the sinner to recognize his own condition. It conveys, at least potentially, the refusal of the Christian to accept his own need for conversion.

To the extent to which Christian responsibility is involved in it, the tempest that fell on the Jewish people is at the same time a judgement that has fallen on the Christian world. It has shown up the limits of the penetration of the gospel into our consciences after nineteen centuries of Christianity.

The genocide occurred in a society in which the Church had propagated her teaching for over a millennium. Doubtless the history of the Church cannot be reduced to her relations with the synagogue. It would be dishonest to refuse to see the fruits of conversion which the gospel has produced among the nations. It would be simplistic and contrary to the truth to present the history of relations between Christians and Jews as uniformly hostile or malevolent. It would also be unjust not to recall that during the Nazi persecution 'of all human institutions, the Churches saved the greatest number of Jews'.[14] But ultimately we are obliged to admit that the Church, whose vocation it was to manifest reconciliation between Israel and the Gentiles could envisage this reconciliation only through the admission of Jews into her own bosom. Faced with the failure of her preaching, the Church added her own grievances to those of Gentile anti-Semitism, widening the gulf it was her vocation to bridge. In the very heart of the Christian world, nineteen centuries of Christianity did not prevent the greatest attempt to exterminate the Jewish people

---

[14] F. Lovsky and B. Dupuy, Foreword to *Les Eglises devant le judaïsme*, p. 9.

that has ever been known. Must we speak of failure? At any
rate, one thing cannot be doubted: there can be no way out for
us but mercy.

The Identity and the Election of Israel

The Shoah reveals the identity and the election of Israel.

We have already noted that Christian thinking has made
more progress during these past thirty years in its perception of
Judaism than during the preceding nineteen centuries. The fact
is worthy of consideration in its own right. The Shoah, which
reveals by pushing it to its extreme the hardening of the
Gentiles with regard to Israel, is at the same time the shock that
opens our eyes.

In fact, this hardening of the Gentiles with regard to Israel is
no less a mystery than that of the hardening of the Jews with
regard to the gospel. It is easy to understand that the first
generation of Christians, who saw the accomplishment of the
promises in the resurrection of Jesus, were baffled by the
enigma of Israel's failure to recognize its own Messiah. The
situation was entirely unexpected and threw Paul into a state of
painful perplexity, but to an even greater extent it led him into
the adoration of the God whose plans were beyond his
comprehension (Rom. 11.33–6). But if we consider the
implications of the simple fact of adhering to the Christian
faith, we may conclude that in the end the greatest mystery of
all is that faith should be possible. And the Christian should
above all be struck with amazement when he contemplates the
election of which he is the object and the gift he has been given
of believing in what is beyond belief.

The hardening with regard to Israel carries the implication
that the Christian is truly overcome with blindness when
confronted with the Scriptures of which he is the guardian. It is
Scripture itself which forbids him to doubt God's faithfulness to
God's own commitments; it is the New Testament which
reminds him that the gifts of God are irrevocable (Rom. 11.29;

cf. 2 Tim. 2.13) and which acts as an express warning against any temptation of arrogance with regard to Israel (Rom. 11.17–24). This blindness of the Christian is not unrelated to sin; indeed, Christian anti-Semitism, as we have seen, is the symptom of the pagan's refusal of the gospel.

It would be excessively optimistic to say that the Shoah has ended this blindness. The mechanisms of defence are still too strong; there are old habits of thought too solidly established for new insights to be adopted rapidly and without resistance. However, it is undeniable that the Churches have initiated a decisive change and that the genocide has led many Christians to look afresh at the Jewish people. We have seen how history invites us to make an analogy between the sufferings of Israel and the condition of the persecuted Servant related in Scripture.[15] The Shoah shows the identity of Israel to the eyes of the Gentiles and points it out to the world as the suffering Servant.

The word 'shows' is used on purpose. The Shoah does not confer a new title on the Jewish people or a title that was lost after having been granted. The Jewish people is the Servant of the Lord by divine choice and nowhere in the Scriptures do we read that it has lost this identity.[16] On the contrary, the New Testament forcefully affirms that the gifts of God are irrevocable, and Paul, in chs. 9 to 11 of Romans, on three separate occasions designates by the term 'Israel' those Jews who had not adhered to the gospel.[17] If, therefore, the Christian might wish to consider that the Jewish people has been stripped of its election, he has to undertake to prove it against Scripture. On this subject, it is important to note that from biblical times onward the persecutions inflicted by Christians have been those which most painfully recalled to the Jewish people their identity as the suffering Servant. Rashi and Ibn Ezra would probably not

---

[15] Cf. *supra* pp. 20–5.
[16] Isa. 42.1. Cf. *supra* p. 25.
[17] Rom. 11.29; 9.31; 10.19; 11.7. Cf. *infra* p. 124.

have written their commentaries on Isaiah ch. 53, had they not been contemporaries of the great massacres of Jews that accompanied the departure on Crusade. Thus it was Christians themselves who, tragically and unexpectedly, reminded the Jewish people of its true spiritual identity.

If, therefore, the Shoah constitutes here a threshold or a new stage, it is primarily in the Gentiles rather than in Israel that we need to look for the change in the revelation that has led the Gentiles to begin to perceive that to which they had been blind. 'As many people were aghast at him – he was so inhumanly disfigured that he no longer looked like a man – so many nations will be astonished and kings will stay tight-lipped before him, seeing what had never been told them, learning what they had not heard before' (Isa. 52.14–15).

However, seen from Israel's side, the Shoah is far more than a simple unveiling because it represents a singular meeting between history and the prophetic word. And while the Word sheds light on the event – though we must be careful not to imply that the entire significance of the event is clarified without any obscurity remaining – the event in return gives an unheard-of fulfilment to the Word. Therefore, in this encounter between history and the prophetic Word, a new conjunction with its own identity also comes about for Israel.

The Shoah is an epiphany, inverted in some sort since the Servant is revealed in suffering rather than in glory. Epiphany, nonetheless, in which history and the Word agree in their testimony to the Elect of God.

Elect of God because, as we must repeat, it is divine choice and not suffering that consecrates Israel as the Servant of the Lord. It is not because Israel knew suffering that it became the Servant. Quite the reverse, Scripture suggests that it is because it is the Servant that the world's suffering falls on it and, by it, suffering may lose its nonsensical character. It would not, therefore, be justified to give the title of Servant indiscriminately to victims of all and any abuses and injustices. This misuse of the term, which tends to empty it of its meaning, can give rise to a sterile justification of suffering and distress. Such a justification may also be an expression of an attitude which has already been described and which consists in denying any specific character to Jewish existence. Such an attitude expresses the scandal inevitably provoked by God's choice of a particular people for the salvation of the world.[18]

Jewish tradition tells us that as soon as God gave his law to Israel on Mt Sinai 'hatred descended on the idolaters'.[19] The choice that the One God makes of a special people to signify the unique relationship God means to establish with each one of his creatures and to reveal to each person their own uniqueness, is felt first as an inequality and then as an injustice. Is it possible that a certain abstract and impersonal conception of universalism, in the name of which Christians are so quick to declare (against Scripture) that the election of Israel is henceforth obsolescent, does not proceed, at least in part, from the same 'jealousy'? It is a difficult but necessary task to untangle the ideas that emerge from the wish to affirm the Christian faith in as clear a manner as possible, from other ideas which, under the pretence of defending orthodoxy, merely express the resistance with which the Gentiles oppose biblical Revelation and its logic. People do not accept that their equals might be the objects of a special choice. That theme is as old as the relationship between God and humanity; the episode of Joseph and his brothers lives as the eternal parable of it (Gen. 37). Human beings do not willingly accept the gift of God through the mediation of people who are in the fullest sense their fellow creatures. For Christians, who see the Elect of God first, if not exclusively, in the person of Jesus Christ, the scandal of mediation is attenuated, perhaps even unconsciously, by faith in the divinity of Jesus and in the perfection of his humanity. The permanence of the election of Israel reminds us that it is in the

---

[18] Cf. *supra*, p. 13.
[19] *Exodus Rabba* 2.4. The Hebrew word designating 'hatred' (*sinah*) is close to the word Sinai.

choice of an ordinary humanity that all the families of the earth
are blessed by God (cf. Gen. 12.3).

The paradox is that the identity of Israel has been manifested
by a situation which appears precisely to be a refutation of its
election. Here the scandal is intensified before the silence of a
God who does not intervene to save from death the one to
whom he has given his word. Israel thus finds itself plunged
into the situation of all those whose distress appears to witness
against the very existence of God.

But from within this abandonment Israel has never ceased to
worship and praise God, thus maintaining, however mysteri-
ously, communion between God and fallen humanity. Here
again, we must be careful not to apply set phrases to a reality
that obviously goes way beyond what we can grasp of it. But in
this faith and in this communion with God, which the forces of
death have not been able to overcome, we may be allowed to
see a pledge of hope for humanity. From the depths of its
humiliation, Israel kept alive a flame that the powers of darkness
were unable to extinguish.

Even though the election of Israel is laden with ambiguities –
like everything in this world – and shocks our sense of equity
on more than one count, it is a gift which God has given
humanity. Refusing to accept the gift is like putting under a tub
the lamp that can give meaning to the human adventure.

The Relationship of Jesus to Israel

The Shoah, which reveals the identity and the election of Israel,
demonstrates at the same time the permanent relationship
uniting Jesus to his people. If Jesus and the Jewish people share
the same destiny and fulfil the same Scriptures, it is no longer
possible to situate the one over against the other simply in terms
of opposition or to claim that Jesus came to make Israel's
vocation obsolete. Here again, it is appropriate to speak of an
unveiling, for the relationship that now emerges into the full
light of day was already there even if unnoticed. Consequently,

here too, history passes judgement retrospectively not only on the attitude of Christians toward Jews down the centuries but also on habits of thought and language – is 'theology' the right word? – concerning the relationship of Jesus to the Jewish people. The whole way in which Jesus and Israel have been related to each other has been invalidated. From now on, Christian thinking is constrained to renounce certain simplistic and routine conceptions or formulae which do not do justice to the whole of reality.

This applies particularly to the manner of conceiving the fulfilment which the life, death and resurrection of Jesus Christ bring to Judaism. Christian faith affirms that the destiny of Israel was concentrated 'when the time had fully come' (cf. Gal. 4.4) in the person of Jesus who is recognized as the 'Amen' through which God's promises are realized (Rev. 3.14; 2 Cor. 1.20). By his resurrection, Jesus introduced a decisive innovation into history by opening the doors of the kingdom on this earth. But it would be unfair to the Christian faith to reduce the innovation of Jesus Christ to what can be perceived empirically and to conceive the relation of the Old and the New as a purely chronological sequence. Even if it found visible expression in the birth and development of Christianity, it hardly needs to be stated that the fulfilment realized in Jesus Christ is of an order entirely other than the historical succession of two 'religions', the second of which supposedly renders the first obsolete. By his resurrection, Jesus does attain a new mode of existence which places him beyond time and space; from now on time and space are within him. Accordingly, categories of before and after cannot alone render justice to all of the reality which is evoked here. The fulfilment in question is of a quite different order than, for example, the final element of a succession that pushes back into the past everything prior to it, or a 'newness' in the weakest sense, which makes all that has preceded it old-fashioned. Fulfilment recapitulates and gives consistency and fullness of meaning to all that has led up to it. Far from destroying that which it comes to conclude, fulfilment saves the past from obsolescence, giving it eternal value.

Here, the New Testament can enlighten us by the manner by which it perceives the bond between the resurrection of Jesus and his life on earth. Apostolic preaching proclaims first and foremost the coming of the kingdom which is accomplished and manifested in the resurrection of Jesus. Then, commemorating the life on earth of the man from Nazareth, it interprets his life in the light of its end and sees the resurrected Lord in the Jesus of history. By thus identifying Christ with Jesus of Nazareth, it affirms that the resurrection is far from reducing Jesus' life in the flesh to insignificance but, on the contrary, brings it to its final consecration.

Now, between Judaism and the earthly life of Jesus, there is far more than a simple analogy. Judaism is not simply a preparation which finds its culmination in Jesus Christ. Judaism is not anterior but interior to Jesus.[20] The mystery of Christ would be much impoverished by being reduced to what opposes him to the Pharisees of the gospel – in the same way that Judaism would be trivialized by being identified with those of its religious leaders displayed on the stage of the New Testament. Jesus is Jewish. To say this is not simply to make a rather unimportant remark about his ethnic origins, but to define a spiritual identity which is assumed as such into the resurrection.

Avoiding both the temptation to iron out contradictions and the return to closed though reassuring positions which fail to respect the integrity of Christian faith, theology has to search for rigour while refusing to do violence to a reality which cannot be captured in words.

All this, of course, can be perceived and expressed only from within Christian faith, which recognizes in Jesus the one who accomplished the hope of Israel. The Christian must not, therefore, be so naive as to see in the concordance between the destiny of Jesus and that of the Jewish people, an apologetic

[20] See footnote on p. xii.

argument in favour of Christian faith. Nor should he be surprised if the Jew cannot share his convictions or intuitions on this point. On the contrary, he will have the salutary experience of the relative solitude which cannot fail to result from the gift of faith and he will also experience the necessarily asymmetric character of relations between Jews and Christians.

Above all, the Christian must remember that Jesus is truly intelligible only in the light of a Scripture that gives witness also – and indeed first of all – to Israel. Christians who forget this fundamental truth may adopt one of two possible attitudes.

The first attitude is to refer to Jesus Christ as if he represented an entirely new beginning, without roots in any tradition. Under such conditions, the identification of the suffering of Israel with that of Jesus can – and does – elicit the accusation of wanting to annex Judaism, or else of being incapable of experiencing Jewish suffering for what it is and of perceiving it only through that of Jesus. Furthermore, and most of all, it relies on conceptions which very much impoverish Christian faith, indeed actually deprive it of content. Its underlying message is that the person of Jesus, his life, suffering, death and resurrection carry their own meaning quite independently of the Scripture that witnesses to them. In fact, not a single word which Christian faith uses to convey the mystery of Christ has any content outside that given by biblical tradition even if the fulfilment in Jesus Christ gives Scripture in return the fullness of its meaning. But to empty Christology of its biblical content is to open the door to every kind of theory and ideology while closing it to revelation. The very name and title of Jesus Christ have meaning only with reference to one people, one tradition, one Scripture and one hope. Outside these perspectives, to identify Israel with Jesus is not only to invert the normal order of things, but actually to make a statement entirely lacking in content.

The second attitude consists in expressing oneself as if Scripture designated the person of Jesus directly, independently of the people to which he belonged. Or what ultimately comes to the same thing, as if Jesus had concentrated in himself the meaning of Scripture in such a way that Israel were thenceforth cut off from it. But such a concept of the fulfilment supposes that Jesus is to be situated in relation to his people uniquely in terms of chronological succession. We have seen that this conception does not do justice to Christian faith itself.

According to either conception, the application of Scripture to Israel would be possible only at the price of extending the meaning of a Word, which of itself would designate Jesus Christ first of all. Now to recognize Jesus as Servant is to affirm that he leads to its fulfilment a Scripture which first and foremost and quite rightly refers to Israel. The Christian has no business therefore to be generously giving back to the Jewish people something which Jesus never took from them. To stress this is not to diminish Jesus but to make him comprehensible by situating him within the tradition in which the words acquire a meaning.

The first Christians coming from Judaism discovered in Jesus the one who led the Scriptures to their fulfilment. It still remains for the disciple coming from the Gentiles to search more deeply into what that Scripture is that Jesus comes to accomplish, the tradition in which it was elaborated, the spiritual adventure it expresses and the meaning of the vocation of the people in which the Word is embodied.

The Situation of Christians in Relation to Jesus Christ

If the Shoah unveils the identity of Israel to the eyes of the Gentiles and throws light on the bond between Jesus and his people, there is a final ineluctable corollary: the attitude of Christians toward the Jews reveals the reality of their own situation in relation to Jesus.

That is true first of all in the name of the straightforward solidarity that unites Jesus to those close to him and which has been summed up by Barth in a lapidary phrase: 'The Jewish problem is the problem of Christ.' Recalling that Jesus Christ cannot be disassociated from Israel does not imply a denial of his lordship nor does it diminish his irreducible singularity. 'All you have done to one of these little ones who are my brothers, you have done to me' (Matt. 25.40). After the Shoah, the resonance of these words in the mouth of the Jew Jesus is unbearable.

But it is not only in its ultimate results that Christian hostility toward the Jews is revealed as directed at Christ himself. As we have already said, it is in its essence that Christian anti-Semitism reveals the pagan's refusal of the gospel or, at the very least, his resistance to it. Christian anti-Semitism expresses in a special way the attitude of dodging the appeal to conversion by designating the other as the one to whom the appeal is first addressed, or indeed of exonerating oneself by transferring one's own responsibilities onto others. In traditional Christian typology for obvious reasons the Jew tends to personify humanity's refusal of Christ and to symbolize all that is an obstacle to the gospel.[21] By designating the Jew as Christ's adversary, the Christian puts himself by his own authority on the side of the faithful and the innocent. There is something derisory (and I shall have to recur to this) in a certain manner of identifying or associating everything opposed to the gospel with Judaism, thus excluding the condition of sinfulness from a Christianity which is idealized but wholly illusory. To make the Jew the personification of opposition to Christ is to identify oneself with the Pharisee of the parable and, by a total inversion of the gospel message, to take pride in one's faith and glory in one's righteousness.

But to the extent that anti-Semitism reaches its own logical conclusion in violence, the circle is complete and the contradiction blatant: the death of the Jew represents a tragic denial of the Gentile's protestations of righteousness and innocence.

[21] In order to be convinced of this, we need only observe the symbolic value which still is attached today to terms such as 'Law', 'circumcision', 'Sabbath', 'synagogue', 'Pharisee', even 'Old Testament' in Christian teaching as expressed in catechesis, theology and the liturgy.

Seen from this angle, the Shoah again plays a revelatory role. Of course in this domain even more than in others over-simplification and caricature must be avoided. There is no need to repeat that the terrible fate reserved for the Jewish people during the present epoch goes way beyond what can be laid to the account of Christian responsibility, which has certainly not been exercized in one direction only. Nonetheless there can be no denying the part which the reasons evoked above have played, directly or not, in the misfortunes suffered by the Jewish people. In this respect, on the scale of humanity, the event takes on the meaning and the clarity of an immense parable. It reveals the effects of mechanisms at work in the consciousness of every person. The Jews are far from being the sole victims of such mechanisms although these latter have rarely been seen to act so clearly.

Should any Christian be likely to forget it, the Shoah is a reminder of how hard it is to accept the gospel for what it is: a power for inner transformation. Not to accept it in such a way and to dodge the appeal to conversion means to empty the gospel of its content and transform Christianity into a doctrine and the Church into a mere institution. But under such conditions, to glory in one's faith in Christ and to look for the justification of one's good conscience by searching the gospel means in reality to put oneself beyond redemption, rejecting Christ and 'putting the Son of God back on the cross' (Heb. 6.6). Thus the ambiguity in the condition of the Christian becomes clear: he appeals to an ideal, according to which he can only be found wanting, he commends himself to a Christ whom he constantly denies, he is rich only in the mercy given him on condition that he be willing to receive it. Brutally and irrefutably, history demonstrates here that recognizing Jesus as Lord is less a matter of displaying one's own merits than of recognizing one's need for salvation.

5

Questions

We are left perplexed when reflection on the Shoah shows us how few traces the most sinister event in the history of humanity seems to have left in our theology. Christian thinking over recent decades seems to have given far more attention to questions posed by scientific and technological progress, development, political life, sexuality, the encounter between faith and the humanities. As we have already said, the excessive scale and absurdity of the genocide make it impossible to try to write anything logical or sensible about the subject. But it would be sheer blindness on our part to think that because we are dealing with a reality that does not allow itself to be expressed in words, the genocide is therefore insignificant and can be simply ignored. And yet it is not certain that the importance of the event is recognized even implicitly in our affirmations, or that the silence between our words is perceptible. On the contrary, it is hard to guard ourselves against the feeling that we have gone on thinking and talking as if nothing had happened in certain fundamental issues where our words ought to bear the mark of the questions raised by the genocide. Does this come from a desire to chase a nightmare out of our memories by telling ourselves that the genocide belongs only to the past? Or are we convinced that we have better things to do today than to go on reflecting about an event which we think, quite unwarrantedly, cannot recur? Are we afraid of the terrifying questions the event would not fail to raise, should we agree not to dodge it? But can we allow ourselves to skirt around this nonsensical faultline which has opened up in the midst of our convictions and certainties paying no attention when the simple fact that it could happen is in essence a threat to the very legitimacy of our affirmations?

Having said that, an escalation of self-criticism or reassessments cannot *ipso facto* render justice to the importance of the event.

There are present-day Christian theologians who detect the distant origin of the genocide in the very wording of our faith and who recommend nothing less than the elaboration of a new Christology in order to put an end to anti-Semitism.[1] It is true that recent history obliges us to search for and recognize our own responsibility in the suffering endured by the Jewish people. But it is far from clear that in order to undertake this kind of study, the best way to orient oneself is to begin by destroying the landmarks ... In reality, emptying Christology of its content has less to do with repentance than with self-destruction. If Christianity were to start by denying its own substance, what kind of 'dialogue' could it undertake with Judaism?[2]

There seems then to be a choice between on the one hand a silence that arouses suspicion that it betrays a fear of facing up to questions, and on the other a radicalism which may mask a suicidal refusal to take on a Christian identity under the guise of courage and lucidity.

But isn't this narrow path precisely that of faith?

Asking such a question does not imply that faith could bring some miraculous solution to insoluble problems. On the

[1] R. R. Ruether wonders whether it is possible to say: 'Jesus is the Messiah' without at the same time affirming explicitly or implicitly: 'The Jews are condemned'. The same author states: 'Our theological critique of Christian anti-Judaism ... must turn to what was always the other side of anti-Judaism, namely Christology.' R. R. Ruether, *Faith and Fratricide: The Theological Roots of Anti-Semitism* (New York: Seabury Press, 1974), p. 246.

[2] 'No Jew in his right mind will seek an encounter with a triumphalist Church, neither can he be interested in a conversation with a Christian about to commit suicide.' J. M. Osterreicher, *Anatomy of Contempt: A Critique of R. R. Ruether's 'Faith and Fratricide'* (The Institute of Judeo-Christian Studies, Seton Hall University, South Orange, New Jersey, 1975), p. 37.

contrary, it involves bearing in mind that the believing condition – and this is both its privilege and its fragility – obliges us to venture beyond the firm ground of proofs and immediate certitude (Matt. 14.28–31), that faith for us humans consists in taking up the challenges that God throws at us in face of the impossible (Ezek. 37.3), that the Word of God may come to constitute the only light for the believer when there are no other landmarks, that this Word is a call endlessly dislodging us from a facile security and certainty.

If, therefore, the believer is led to ask himself a certain number of questions, he must seek the answers from within the Christian faith rather than in opposition to it.

The Silence of God

'Where was he [God] when Hitler did what no man should ever have done?'[3] When asked by a Jew, the question is not an academic one and if it has to be tackled now, it is not with the pretension of adding yet another paragraph to the discourse on the theme of the 'death of God'.

We have already invoked the enigma and the scandal constituted by the passivity of a God who does not intervene but allows the death of those to whom he has pledged himself in the Covenant. Given that the chosen people are involved, this is the way in which the problem has to be stated first of all, even if it does not come naturally to the mind of the Christian, who may be used to thinking about the question of the presence and the action of God in history more generally and less personally. After Auschwitz, what meaning have the assurances which God heaps on the one who puts his trust in him? 'They will carry you in their arms so that you will not strike your foot against a stone ... He will call upon me and I will answer him' (Ps. 91.12, 15). At first sight, in the light of the

---

[3] E. B. Borowitz, *How Can a Jew Speak of Faith Today?* (Philadelphia: Westminster Press, 1969), p. 33.

death camps, such words cannot seem to be anything but
tragically derisory; we are all too well aware that no platitude on
liberty or 'the problem of evil' can really resolve the enigma.
Before the gigantic absurdity of Auschwitz the best-established
certainties can waver and it would be more than a little shallow
to show astonishment or indignation at the opinion that
something in the relationship between God and humankind has
henceforth been irremediably shattered. It is true that the
question put to God by the believer who feels abandoned by
him is not new in the tradition of Israel; Scripture bears witness
to it (Ps. 22). But in the Shoah there is something totally new,
both in nature and in scale, and even the spiritual experience of
the silence of God may seem inadequate in the face of it.
Richard Rubenstein writes:

> No man can really say that God is dead. How can we know
> that? Nevertheless, I am compelled to say that we live in the
> time of 'the death of God'. This is more about man and his
> culture than about God. The death of God is a cultural fact.
> Buber felt this. He spoke of the eclipse of God ... When I
> say that we live in the time of the death of God, I mean that
> the thread uniting God and man, heaven and earth has been
> broken. We stand in a cold, silent, unfeeling cosmos unaided
> by any purposeful power beyond our resources. After
> Auschwitz what else can a Jew say about God?[4]

It is true that this assertion is somewhat dated as an analysis of a
cultural phenomenon but we cannot but register it as bearing
witness to the experience of its author. Yet we also need to
register the fact that such an attitude is not the only one
possible; in the eclipse of God the believer can see a challenge to
be taken up by faith.

Emil Fackenheim writes:

> Jews are forbidden to hand Hitler posthumous victories.

[4] R. L. Rubenstein, *After Auschwitz. Radical Theology and Contemporary
Judaism*, (New York: Bobbs-Merrill, 1966), pp. 151–2.

They are forbidden to despair of the God of Israel lest Judaism perish. A religious Jew who has stayed with his God may be forced into new, possibly revolutionary relationships with Him. One possibility, however, is totally unthinkable. A Jew may not respond to Hitler's attempts to destroy Judaism by himself co-operating in its destruction.[5]

The ways of the religious Jew are revolutionary, for there has never been a Jewish protest against divine power like this protest. Continuing to hear the voice of Sinai as he hears the voice of Auschwitz, in his citing God against God, he may have to assume extremes that dwarf those of Abraham, Jeremiah, Job and Rabbi Levi Yitzhak. ('You have abandoned the Covenant? We shall not abandon it! You no longer want Jews to survive? We shall survive as better, more faithful, more pious Jews! You have destroyed all grounds for hope? We shall obey the commandment to hope which You Yourself have given!'[6]). A modern paraphrase of Job's profession of faith: 'Job served the Holy One, blessed be He, only in love as it is said: Though he slay me, yet will I hope in him. (Job, 13.15).'[7]

Here we had to let the witnesses speak. This is no place to judge in general, abstract terms between two personal convictions. Since we are dealing with subjective attitudes, without giving this term the derogatory sense it often has, such arbitration would be meaningless. The fact remains that after Auschwitz some people are unable to believe in a personal God acting in history. As Rubenstein emphasizes, such a conclusion is more of a statement about humankind than a statement about God. It is also a fact that the survivors include people whose faith was not destroyed. We cannot doubt the sincerity of any of them and it can be thought that the position of the former may not seem so strange to the latter who know from experience the depth of the darkness which serves as background to the light of faith.

---

[5] E. L. Fackenheim, *God's Presence in History: Jewish Affirmations and Philosophical Reflections* (New York: Harper & Row, 1970), p. 84.

[6] Fackenheim, *God's Presence in History*, p. 88.

[7] *Mishna Sota*, 5.5.

But as to the question whether it is possible, after Auschwitz, to believe in a personal God present in human history, the fact that believers exist is the only possible answer. The answer may seem fragile and it certainly does not constrain acceptance, as befits everything concerned with faith, but for the person given the gift of faith that answer feels right. When God seems absent, he manifests his power in human hearts by enabling them to believe, love and hope despite all the evidence.

The questions raised by the disappearance of the divine presence in the face of the genocide concern first of all the relations of God with his people. They become most significant within the Covenant. The Jewish people experiences these questions in its own specific way and no outsider can really experience them in the same terms, even if they awaken strong resonances in every believer who has suffered the ordeal of the silence of God on his own account, for it goes without saying that the religious experience of Israel cannot be totally different from the experience of faith in general.

Even so, every believer – and not just the Jew – should be affected by the genocide in his way of conceiving the presence of God. On this point the Shoah should destroy all naive and simplistic conceptions. And here too, it is allowable to remain perplexed in the face of the many forms of a certain kind of providentialism which, only a few decades after Auschwitz, expresses itself as if the presence of God were constantly perceptible and identifiable and his plans immediately and directly intelligible.

'Our faith in God will be purified', writes Eva Fleischner:

> if we suffer the impact of the Holocaust (unless, indeed – and we must admit this possibility – it is destroyed). A glib, easy affirmation that God is good and looks after us all, that all suffering has a deeper purpose, that good always comes from evil – such clichés are no longer possible after Auschwitz. Does this mean that faith in God is no longer possible? I for one do not think so. But such faith will henceforth be lived in alternating moments of darkness and light. Perhaps it has always been so with authentic faith –

the 'dark night of the soul' is after all no 20th century
invention. But the Holocaust accentuates this aspect of
faith.[8]

What Redemption?

The Shoah also forces us to question the content of the
expressions we use when we affirm that the world has been
saved.

In the museum of the Diaspora in Tel Aviv an inscription in
bronze in the hall of the Shoah, recalls that: 'In the year one
thousand nine hundred and thirty-three of the Christian era,
Adolph Hitler came to power in Germany. In his day the
Germans and their accomplices exterminated six million Jews
among which were one and a half million children. Shut away
in the ghettos, the victims fought desperately for their lives
while the world looked on in silence.'

This is not the place to go back and look at the relation of
cause and effect which is implied here, linking the very
existence of Christianity to the extermination of six million
Jews. But should the fact that it is possible to date the greatest
extermination enterprise that the world has ever known on the
calendar of the 'Christian era', not encourage us to wonder
what we mean when we proclaim that death has been
vanquished?[9] Faced with the apparent denial of our affirmation
by the fact, is it enough to emphasize the internal and spiritual
character of redemption or to affirm that salvation is the object

[8] E. Fleischner, 'Holocaust, a Christian view', in *Jerusalem Post,* 8 April
1977, p. 8.

[9] Is it in bad taste to recall a coincidence? It was also in 1933 that the
Catholic Church, on the initiative of Pope Pius XI, celebrated the 'Jubilee of
the Redemption' to mark the 19th centenary of the redemption of the world
and of 'all those admirable blessings which began the true rebirth of the world,
the Christian life and civilisation whose ripened fruit we taste ...' (Pius XI,
Christmas and New Year Wishes, 24 December 1932, Documentation
catholique no. 640, 7 January 1933, col. 15).

of faith? Doesn't recent history oblige us to highlight in our theology of redemption the importance of hope for the fullness of a salvation which is yet to come? Without fear of being suspected of 'Judaization' or of falling into millenarism, can one point out that according to the New Testament, the creation itself lives in hope of being liberated from its bondage to decay (Rom. 8.21)?

Let us add that to revive Christian hope and, in a way, reorientate the theology of salvation in the direction of 'not yet', is to share communion to a certain extent with Jewish hope.

After what has befallen Israel, the Christian should have no difficulty in understanding that the Jew cannot see the way in which Christianity has written itself into history as the accomplishment of the messianic promise or that, by refusing to be satisfied with the world as it is, and also by refusing to doubt God's faithfulness to his promise, the Jew persists in waiting for the coming of the Messiah 'even though he may tarry'.[10] To see this vigilant wait for a visible salvation as linked to the 'blessed hope' (Titus 2.13) of the Christian for the manifestation of the Saviour is not to succumb to the lure of the false analogy. Our hope becomes all the more poignant when we see our own errors and experience our own need for salvation. Here the threads join up: our acknowledgement of our wrongdoing toward the people of Israel leads us, by robbing us of all arrogance towards them to turn with them toward the salvation which comes from God.

Other questions emerge from the contrast between the perspectives opened up by the New Testament and a realization of what really has happened over the two millennia of Church history.

---

[10] 'I believe with perfect faith in the coming of the Messiah and even though he may tarry, I wait daily for his coming.' Extract from the 13 articles of faith of Maimonides.

What Jealousy?

Faced with the refusal by the Jewish people as a whole to listen to the preaching of the gospel, Paul decided to turn to the pagans, claiming that he hoped to 'arouse the envy of his own people' (Rom. 11.14; cf. 11.11). From Paul's perspective, the gospel should have produced in the Gentiles the fruits that it had not produced in Israel; the spiritual vitality manifested by the pagans should have brought about that which Apostolic preaching had not been able to achieve, namely to reveal the power of the gospel to the eyes of the Jews.

Nineteen centuries after the Epistle to the Romans, what judgement can be passed on the way these perspectives have materialized? What fruits has the gospel produced in the Gentiles such as to arouse the envy of the Jews? At the risk of being repetitive, it has to be said that a very careful answer has to be given to these questions. It is not possible to draw up a balance sheet for two thousand years in a few lines and the answer to the question cannot really be given by Christians. However, the formidable question does remain and it should not be answered evasively or superficially: how has it come about that the fruits which Christianity has produced among the Gentiles as far as the Jews are concerned, have been so full of bitterness and death?

What Reconciliation?

A question very close to this one concerns the attitude of the Gentile-Christians to the Jews, first toward the Judaeo-Christians within the Church itself in Antiquity and then, as the Church and Israel drew further and further apart, toward the Jewish people. The problem has been mentioned above[11] but must be addressed explicitly here because it concerns a

---

[11] See pp. 37 and 57.

question to which faith cannot remain indifferent and which theology cannot be allowed to avoid: the Church understands herself as the visible realization of the unity of Jews and Gentiles united together by Christ in one body. So how has it come about that the Church has so often played a contrary role and has aggravated the division she was supposed to overcome? The first answer we can give is the one Paul gave when he was confronted with another enigma: 'It is not as though God's word had failed' (Rom. 9.6). Whatever may have been the history of the relations between the Church and the Jewish people, Jesus has in his own flesh made the two one (cf. Eph. 2.14). The Church has never ceased to bring Jews and Gentiles together, whatever ambiguities there may have been in the manner of conceiving this unity and in the situation of the 'converts' within the Church. But this affirmation leaves aside the question raised by the contrast between the mystery of the Church – in the proper sense of the word, that is to say her spiritual reality – and the visible expression of it, at least in relation to what concerns us here. How can the Church, which defines herself as a sacrament that is to say as the sign and instrument of the spiritual reality she bears,[12] have managed to express herself so often, in her acts as in her teaching, in a manner so far removed from her own definition?

The Word of God and History

The simple fact that such questions can be asked leads to another which touches on the theology of history: how can the word of God be thus belied and his plan of salvation so massively held in check? The question is not new. It covers much of the same terrain as that of the relation between the will of God and human liberty. But the implications and significance of the Shoah give it a dimension and a sharpness

---

[12] Vatican II, Constitution *Lumen Gentium*, chap. 1, para. 1.

that are almost unprecedented. The problem raised here goes far beyond the debate on the way in which the liberty of the individual can orientate itself according to the plan of God, or be opposed to it.

Faced with this apparent failure of the power of God, the believer should not be taken by surprise, for Scripture knows the strength of the resistance which the work of the redemption of the world must encounter.[13] Here again, in brutally reminding us of certain truths, the facts force us to shift the centre of gravity in our teaching. It is difficult to see how, without averting our eyes from reality, we can conceive the coming of the kingdom as the culmination of a continual progress in the well-being and the moral consciousness of humanity.

Questions for Tradition and the Theology of History

There are two questions that have been running parallel to the preceding reflections and which have to do with the theology of history, and they now need to be expressed explicitly.

The first concerns the unique character of the Shoah.[14] Can we admit that 'in our time, the final days' (Heb. 1.2), in these last times inaugurated by the resurrection of Jesus Christ, an event qualitatively new, and therefore unprecedented of its kind, can have happened?

Again, rigour must be a priority. Without emptying the Christian faith of its content, it is inadmissible to allow the possibility of any event on a level with the paschal mystery of Christ, and consequently attenuate the unique character of that mystery.[15] But might the unfolding of what was inaugurated in Jesus Christ take place in stages? Is it necessary to hold that a 'sacred history', each phase of which is given meaning in terms

---

[13] See for instance the Revelation to John.
[14] Cf. *supra*, pp. 42–50.
[15] Cf. Vatican II, Constitution *Dei Verbum*, no. 4.

of the prophetic word, is followed by an ecclesiastical history, the general significance of which comes from the New Testament though none of its principal events is susceptible of a specific interpretation from the point of view of faith? Here once more we touch upon the theme of a debate which is hardly new and which goes well beyond the subject of these reflections. Without straying beyond the limits of our subject, it is at least relevant to remark that, according to Scripture, the relation that unites or separates Jews and Gentiles constitutes one of the fundamental structures in the history of salvation, since the redemption of humankind depends on the reconciliation of Israel and the nations. It is, therefore, legitimate to see theological significance in everything that affects this relationship on the one side or the other. Now, as we have seen, in this area the Shoah constitutes a decisive threshold in two ways. With unprecedented violence and clarity, it expresses the rejection of Israel by the Gentiles, while at the same time constituting a point of departure for the Gentiles in the opposite direction, marking their passage from hardening to recognition, in the sense and within the limits described above. There is justification for the recognition that recent events and their consequences – insofar as the reciprocal relations of Jews and Gentiles have been modified by them – represent a stage in the history of redemption of humanity.

The second question is still more delicate: what use can we or should we make of Christian tradition on Judaism? This is an inevitable question for a Christian meditating on the Shoah as soon as we admit some responsibility on the part of Christians, including the Doctors of the Church, for the existence of a climate of anti-Semitism without which the genocide could not have taken place. Even if we cannot claim to be able to answer the question, we can at least attempt to define our terms. What normative character can we attribute to a teaching which, only too often since the patristic era, has done nothing but incite malice toward Jews?

At this point we probably need to define what is meant by tradition. It is surely not a good idea to take as rules of faith, for example, comfortably and routinely simplistic statements or invectives resulting from polemics in which jealousy and resentment have held as much place as a disinterested search for the truth. The remark is probably valid to a greater or lesser extent for the patristic interpretation of certain of the great themes of Christian theology. However, traditional teaching on Judaism, insofar as it may be considered to form a coherent whole (not necessarily the case[16]), appears to present a special problem. This is because the formulae and traditional themes, by and in themselves, do not direct us toward satisfactory answers to questions raised by the encounter with contemporary Judaism.

Faced with this situation, several possible attitudes may be imagined.

One would be to confer the stamp of authority to the formulae and themes most commonly met in patristic literature. In so doing, the wish to find a consensus between the Fathers would run the risk of projecting a false uniformity onto the teaching and practices of the early centuries, overlooking differences due to place, time and literary genre. According to this hypothesis, ideas such as the 'rejection' of Israel or the substitution of a 'new' Israel for the old one, which would thereby be deprived of its own election, should be considered as truths of faith to which the Christian would in conscience be bound to adhere.[17] But can we make an abstract dissociation

---

[16] Cf. Simon, *Verus Israel*, pp. 87–124, 166–88, 239–74.

[17] 'The Didascalia expresses ... forcefully and clearly the principle that we have already seen emerging in the most ancient authors and which are repeated unanimously by Tradition: the total and definitive loss of Israel's privileges which have from then on passed to the Church. This represents a constant of Christian thought; no exceptions are to be found.' (Judant, *Judaïsme et Christianisme*, pp. 151–2. 'At no time did the Fathers believe that the verse of St. Paul: "There is no change of mind on God's part about the gifts he has made or of his choice" could apply to the unbelieving part of the Jewish people and we do not hesitate to emphasise that on this point, which constitutes an interpretation of Scripture, there is unanimous agreement between the Fathers' (p. 262). 'It is true that the concept of a "mystery of Israel" is foreign to them [the Fathers of the Church]. But is this not proof that this new concept is not in the line of Tradition?' (p. 271).

between this 'tradition' and the fruit it has borne? And above all, what authority can be attributed to expressions so far removed from a Scripture they are supposed to explain and actualize? The option chosen by the Second Vatican Council on this subject is enough to alert us to the existence of a real problem here.[18] The fact that Vatican II did not refer to any authority beyond that of Scripture in its text on Judaism is specially remarkable, considering the care the Council took to show how its teaching fitted in with the continuity of the tradition of the Church even when it was dealing with relatively new themes.[19] The silence of the Council on the teaching of the Fathers concerning Judaism is therefore a deliberate choice and far from insignificant. It might be risky to conclude that this silence represents purely and simply a disavowal of tradition. But we are entitled to affirm that on the first occasion when the Church wanted to deal with Judaism in ways other than fragmentary, occasional or polemical, the *sensus fidelium* of which the Council was the interpreter could not be expressed in terms inherited from the past.

Does this mean that we should simply ignore our ecclesiastical heritage concerning Judaism? That would be an error as grave as the former, for several quite different kinds of reason.

The first has to do with plain honesty. The teaching and practice of the Church concerning Judaism are intertwined within a patrimony in which the best and the worst are mixed together. What right has the Church of today to refuse to bear the most troublesome part of what former generations have bequeathed her? This is all the truer in that Christian attitudes toward Jews over the past centuries are theologically highly significant.

---

[18] Cf. *supra* pp. 19–20.

[19] Texts like the decrees on ecumenism or religious liberty include references to patristic sources. It should also be remarked that the Council succeeded in introducing a quotation from Gregory VII in the text on Islam (*Nostra Aetate*, no. 3).

The second reason is of another kind. If the Church holds that the expression of her own faith can be elaborated only within the living tradition,[20] would it not in fact be rather arbitrary to challenge the teaching of past centuries on one single important point? By what right and according to which criteria could a specific domain be subtracted thus from the authority of tradition? Strictly from the point of view of theological methodology, the fact of arbitrarily allowing such an exception would create more problems than it would solve.

Above all, let us not forget that a negation is often no more than the reverse of an affirmation: traditional expressions about Judaism – which can only be spoken of in general terms by ignoring nuances of time and style – are often simply the negative face of affirmations that the Church claims for herself. Controversial though the expression 'the new Israel' may be, and dangerous though the consequences that may be drawn from it are, there is no doubt that by using it the Church claims that she is defined by her biblical heritage. Many illustrations of this sort could be cited. There may be vital elements of truth in expressions which rightly shock us, especially bearing in mind what the Jewish people have suffered throughout the centuries and the excesses and aberrations these expressions have inspired. There is no reason why we should relinquish such fragments of truth. And if we must, in the words of Father Y. Congar, follow the truth right up to its boundary with error, we cannot exclude from our tradition that part of the truth which may be mixed in with tares.

Our conclusion must be that in this domain more than in others, tradition cannot be received as it stands and without hermeneutic endeavour.

When doing such work, it must first of all be remembered that tradition is not primarily a code of truths to be believed; the homilies of the Fathers, exegetic commentaries, the invectives of Chrysostom, Byzantine liturgical formularies and the

---

[20] Constitution *Dei Verbum*, chap. 2.

decisions of the mediaeval councils on the status of the Jews should not in themselves be considered as definitive formulations of the Christian faith that have to be taken literally.

It also needs to be remembered that it is only gradually that the Church comes to the perception and expression of her own faith;[21] such a progression in the discovery of the contents of the faith and its implications is not necessarily constant and linear but may actually make occasional quantum leaps. In the life of the Church, as in that of individuals, a specific aspect of truth can be given new significance by history and both internal and external circumstances; awareness of it can be sharpened and fresh light thrown on its implications. There is no need to repeat the reasons why twentieth-century Christians have been newly sensitized to questions raised by the permanence of Judaism.

Finally, we must remember that truth cannot be affirmed without obstacles being overcome that are not all of an intellectual character. In the elaboration of the formulae in which theology is expressed, the intelligence of the believer has to wrestle with words and concepts to attain an ever less imperfect expression of the content of the faith. In the words it uses, living tradition will always bear the mark of the resistances which have had to be overcome in arriving at statements that are as faithful as possible to what they mean to express. But in research of this kind, the believer has to confront a resistance other than that of language or formulae, and that is the conscious or unconscious desire for protection against truths that are anything but comfortable. In the case of reflection on the permanence of Judaism this resistance is particularly sensitive. On this point, our tradition bears not so much the mark of the trials and errors which any patient and disinterested search for truth must necessarily pass through, as the continual reluctance of Gentiles to recognize the election of Israel. This may be why our Christian heritage does not in this field

---

[21] *Dei Verbum*, no. 8.

manifest a harmonious and continuous progress from its inception up to the time of Vatican II. It seems even as if the general movement, rather than showing progressive enlightenment, was one of degeneration and hardening until the shock of the Shoah made us realize how untenable were the traditional formulae concerning the Jews. This is a sign that anti-Judaism, a permanent temptation for the Church and for every believer, is linked in some structural way to the difficulty of accepting the gospel and its implications.

In studying Christian tradition on Judaism, it is possible and indeed it is our duty to look for statements foreshadowing in content and in form those heard more and more frequently in today's Churches.[22] Such affirmations, which may be more frequent than is generally thought, would be witnesses to the fact that the Church never fell completely into aberration in her perception of Judaism and that notions rediscovered today as fundamental were never completely forgotten. However, it would be a bad method to isolate fragments of tradition by tearing them away from a context itself massively opposed to them, since this context also possesses a significance that the Church owes it to herself to analyse carefully in the light of Scripture. From the theological point of view it is both important and significant that the collective memory of the Christian world retains traces of a deep reluctance to recognize the plan of God in the election of Israel. It signifies that anti-Semitism cannot be reduced to bad habits of thought or language which must be eliminated, but is the sign of a real spiritual temptation linked by its very nature to the Christian identity: 'Anti-Semitism is the shadow carried by the mystery of Israel in the rebellious heart of man.'[23] Revelation would lose a large part of its meaning if all the passages not regarded as 'edifying' in the common sense of the term, were to be expurged from the Bible. It would be an error to tear out those

---

[22] Without, however, wanting to find in the Fathers precise answers to the questions we ask ourselves today . . .

[23] Lovsky, *Antisémitisme et mystère d'Israël*, p. 402.

pages of our history that bear witness to the tenacity of the temptation to anti-Semitism in Christian consciences.

Vatican II did not opt to appeal to tradition in its document on Judaism. Without a doubt it was necessary at that time for the Church to show that she did not feel bound by a past that must be disavowed today. But it is doubtful whether theological reflection can really advance unless it takes as its point of departure the respective positions of Jews and of Christians, unless it tries to identify and analyse the trends manifested in them, and unless the Church, far from ignoring her own patrimony, shows a willingness to accept and interpret it with all its lights and shadows.

✡ ✡ ✡

When Paul, in ch. 11 of Romans referred to what he called the 'false step' of the Jews, it was in order to warn the Gentile-Christians against the temptation of arrogance toward Israel. By boasting about what they had received by grace, they would simply be imitating behaviour they were so complacently denouncing. History has amply demonstrated that the warning was not superfluous, neither was the danger illusory. For nearly two millennia the Gentiles too have been taking their 'false steps' and the Jews are the ones who have been paying the price.

Taking the warning seriously means recognizing our share of responsibility for the past; it means admitting that history bears the marks of the use we have made of our liberty; it means ridding ourselves of the simplistic notion (unexpressed but present confusedly in our minds) that though the dangers of falling and of faithlessness were inherent in the 'first' covenant, the Christian is protected from every error of any consequence; and it means understanding that Paul's warning was not a mere empty phrase but was intended to alert us to a real and serious danger.

It also means acknowledging our responsibility for the present and for the future. Here we come back to the theme of an ancient quarrel between Jews and Christians. Jews have been quick to criticize the Christian conception of a free salvation and have accused Christians of finding justification for irresponsibility in the theology of pardon and grace. On their side, Christians have accused Jews of voluntarism and have denounced a conception of salvation by works that over-emphasizes what depends on human liberty. Perhaps we may have to develop a sense of true responsibility and realize that the Passover of Christ represents a basis for a reconciliation that we are called to engage in as a task we have to make our own. Here it is especially incumbent on us to search out the significance of the latent or explicit anti-Judaism so often noticeable in our teaching. We must also take this study to its logical conclusion not only by combating anti-Semitism, but – and this is a task much vaster than expurging anti-Semitism from our manuals – by seeking how to integrate in a positive manner an acknowledgement of the existence and significance of Judaism into the expression of our Christian faith.

Recognizing our responsibility also means realizing its limits. The Nazi genocide not only went well beyond anything that can fairly be blamed on Christianity; it also went far beyond all that can be attributed to mere human responsibility.

The Jewish people have been witness to a mystery of evil that largely eludes the grasp of human intelligence and exceeds anything that can be attributed to human free-will.

Witness to evil; but also in its very abasement and by the manner in which it experienced it, witness to the presence of God. Once more we are confronted with realities that we must beware of turning into formulae. It is Israel itself who forbids us to despair of God and it is the same Word which makes us see the sufferings of the Servant in those of the Jewish people while preventing us from leaving the last word to absurdity.

> If he gives his life as a sin offering,
> he will see his offspring
> and prolong his life,
> and through him Yahweh's good pleasure will be done (Isa. 53.10).

PART 3

Our Relationship with Israel

6

Beyond Perfunctory Contrasts

What images and associations of ideas do themes linked to Judaism bring to mind nowadays in current Christian teaching?

Since the Second World War, and more particularly since the Second Vatican Council as far as Catholics are concerned, ecclesiastical authorities have repeatedly uttered a series of warnings against using certain simplistic and routine ways of thinking that all too summarily set Judaism in opposition to Christianity in order to highlight the person of Christ and the novelty of the gospel.

What impact have these recommendations really had? A serious answer to this question would require a search through all the theological, catechetic, liturgical and homiletic literature of these past decades. But an ordinary reading of a few significant documents reveals the persistence of a certain number of particularly harsh clichés, which seem to be very deeply embedded in Christian habits of thought and language.

Images of Judaism in Christian Teaching
Liturgy – Liturgical Commentaries

For the immense majority of Christians the liturgy constitutes the principal, if not the only occasion when they hear about the Jewish world in the midst of which Christianity was born. To the Christian imagination, Pharisees, scribes, Sabbath, Mosaic Law, synagogue, all make up the religious landscape within which the preaching of the gospel first took place. Missals in use by the faithful, together with their commentaries introducing the biblical readings, are therefore an especially important field of observation for our subject. Now, if most missals show an evident desire to present Judaism in an honest and subtle light, it is unfortunate that the same observation is very far from applicable to the entirety of contemporary liturgical literature. There is no need to spend long hours in study to find, even today, references to Judaism that yield nothing to the classic examples of the genre. As an example, here is an introduction to the parable of the house built on sand (Matt. 7.24–7):

> In a country in which rivers suddenly become swollen after the rain and turn into impetuous torrents, the comparison made by Jesus is striking. But it is all the more so for a people who had thought they had built themselves an impregnable fortress, that of Jerusalem, and who saw it fall, undermined by an inner disease. Even the religion on which they had intended to establish the national edifice, was found to be gangrenous.[1]

Such is the state of the religious world in which Jesus exercized his ministry. Judaism, according to Paul,

> did not recognize the true sense of the divine call. The relation of Israel to God continued to be marked by a mercenary conception of religious life; in exchange for scrupulous observance of the Law, people will obtain divine benevolence and final success.[2]

Mercenary: one of the most frequently used epithets for describing the religion of Israel. The religious system of the Law

---

[1] Emmaus Weekday Missal, in French (10 vols., Paris: Desclée De Brouwer, 1980), vol. 9, p. 178.
[2] Emmaus Sunday Missal, in French (Paris: Desclée De Brouwer, 1979), p. 864. The aim of this commentary is to summarize Rom. 10.8–13.

claims to pay respect to God. But it makes him into a tyrant counting up men's debts and assets. It is a false god constructed by man's mercenary mentality.[3]

The ancient rules of Israel as interpreted by the scribes and Pharisees ... depended essentially on a tit-for-tat mentality.[4]

Scribes and Pharisees are

incapable of opening themselves up to an understanding of God. They are locked into a thought system in which every act is viewed as a part of a bargaining process.[5]

On this point there is no fundamental difference between the Pharisees and the Sadducee priests, their adversaries. What the former claimed to obtain by observance of the Law, the latter want to receive in exchange for sacrifices:

The mercenary mentality displayed in the Temple at Jerusalem concerning the sacrifices is a visible expression of how a certain ritualism has distorted the image of God. He has become the partner in a market ruled by the law of tit-for-tat.[6]

They [the Pharisees] have bought up the Divine Word just as the Sadducees have bought up the Temple. Jesus rebels against them in the name of the living God.[7]

If the religious life of Israel has become degraded to such a degree, the blame essentially lies with the Pharisees, who have 'brought about a veritable perversion of religion'.[8]

---

[3] Emmaus Sunday Missal, p. 1018.
[4] Emmaus Weekday Missal, vol. 4, p. 77.
[5] Emmaus Weekday Missal, vol. 4, p. 111.
[6] Emmaus Sunday Missal, p. 508.
[7] Emmaus Weekday Missal, vol. 3, p. 142.
[8] Emmaus Weekday Missal, vol. 7, p. 33.

Because they are rotten within, the hypocritical scribes and Pharisees have perverted the Jewish tradition. They have turned it into a mercenary system.[9]

The Judaism known by Jesus witnesses to a tradition that was 'formerly living but now fossilized'.[10]

Is there any need to quote the 'narrow racial visions of sectarian Judaism',[11] the 'bursting old wineskins' to which is reduced the religious world of the Pharisees,[12] 'the religion of cheap rubbish',[13] 'the narrow framework of a Judaism incapable of opening itself up to the radiance of universal love',[14] and 'these people imbued with human values marked by ideas of prestige and vengeful force'?[15] There is no point in continuing this list, which contains very few elements capable of counter-balancing this unflattering picture of Judaism at the time of Jesus. There is one allusion to 'simple folk representing the most authentic Jewish piety'.[16] The fact that these simple folk (Simeon and Anna) manifest their piety at that high place of mercenary values, the Temple of Jerusalem, is discreetly passed over. But the general impression that emerges from these pages is that Judaism was almost completely corrupted and perverted, and that the religious ideal of the Old Testament (which is not itself presented in a negative light) had practically dried up at the time of the Christian era, so that the figure of Jesus could be set off to best advantage against the background of a spiritual desert.

As for Jesus, is he truly Jewish?

Nazareth, a remote village in Galilee, is the symbol of a world despised by Jews locked into their elitist world view. It

---

[9] Emmaus Weekday Missal, vol. 7, p. 121.
[10] Emmaus Sunday Missal, p. 633.
[11] Emmaus Weekday Missal, vol. 2, p. 42.
[12] Emmaus Weekday Missal, vol. 2, p. 64.
[13] Emmaus Weekday Missal, vol. 2, p. 20.
[14] Emmaus Weekday Missal, vol. 4, p. 124.
[15] Emmaus Weekday Missal, vol. 10, p. 145.
[16] Emmaus Sunday Missal, p. 457.

was from this village situated in an 'impure' region, that salvation sprang.[17]

As to Israel, she is no more than a barren tree:

The fig tree bearing no more fruit is Israel. The barrenness has become evident in the Temple ... Jesus violently attacks this rotten world doomed to perdition.[18]

Here, no doubt, more than one Christian may feel a certain unease; no matter what the excesses of vocabulary, this is not an invention in all its parts. Isn't it the New Testament itself which denounces religious formalism and which stigmatizes the hypocritical Pharisees and the Temple merchants? If this account of Judaism is untrue to reality, must we conclude that the Evangelists did not know the Jewish world or that Jesus, who 'could tell what someone had within' (John 2.25), could have been so mistaken in his judgement of his contemporaries? And must we pay more attention to the desire to establish cordial relations with the representatives of contemporary Judaism than respect for history?

A Historical Note on Jesus and the Pharisees

It is precisely our concern for historical truth that must dissuade us from taking the Gospel accounts too literally. Without wanting to repeat what has been dealt with much more fully elsewhere,[19] we need to recall briefly certain essential points.

First we must keep in mind the fact that the Gospels are witnesses not only to the life of Jesus before his death, but also to the lives of the first Christian communities at the time of writing. In the accounts of the life of Jesus, we also need to

---

[17] Emmaus Weekday Missal, vol. 2, p. 45.

[18] Emmaus Weekday Missal, vol. 2, p. 213.

[19] See for example Kurt Schubert, *Jésus à la lumière du judaïsme du premier siècle* (*Jesus in the Light of First-Century Judaism*), in French (translated from German by A. Liefooghe; Lectio divina, no. 84; Paris: Cerf, 1974).

know how to read, as in a palimpsest, the continuing testimony of the experiences of the believing community in which the death and resurrection of Jesus were prolonged. What may appear as an anachronism to the modern reader, or as a liberty taken with historical objectivity, is in reality an expression of the faith of the Evangelists: the risen Jesus continues to live in his disciples the drama inaugurated in his earthly life. In his Church he continues to act, to teach, to heal, to offer himself to faith, to meet with incredulity, hostility, persecution. There is no point here in going into material now to be found in every introduction to the New Testament.

Between the time of the death of Jesus and the writing of the Gospels during the final decades of the first century, relations between Christians and the rest of the Jewish community were profoundly modified by the conquest of Jerusalem and the destruction of the Temple. Christians were excluded from the synagogue and their relationship with their former co-religionists became very tense; polemics became far more radical than they had been during Jesus' life on earth. Judaism, for its part, after the catastrophe of the year 70 CE, saw the disappearance of most of the religious currents that had coexisted at the beginning of the century. Only the Pharisees survived, and from now on Judaism would become identified with them.

The Gospels can only reflect this situation. First, by putting into the mouth of Jesus polemical speeches that are far more likely to express the state of relations between Jews and Christians at the end of the first century. Secondly, by categorizing most of the adversaries of Jesus as Pharisees since this term had by now come to be equivalent to that of *Jew*. And yet it is now an established fact that of all the adversaries of Jesus, the Pharisees were by no means the fiercest. K. Schubert notes that some of the criticisms directed by Jesus at the 'hypocritical Pharisees' could in reality only have referred to the Sadducees.[20]

---

[20] Matt. 23.16–22. Schubert, *Jésus,* pp. 50–51.

Moreover, the virulence with which the Evangelists refer to their adversaries was not unusual in the Judaism of the time.

> To understand the violence of the polemics in the Gospels, in particular that of Matthew against the Pharisees, we must remember that arguments between dissident offshoots and the parent body from which they have separated are always extremely vigorous ... If the Pharisees are ... called 'hypocrites' in the gospels, the reproach is far from new. Members of apocalyptic groups used the term against their adversaries who were not equally convinced of the imminence of the great turning-point of history ... The Essenes of Qumran used the term 'hypocritical masters' against their Pharisee adversaries who were noted for realism. So before the time of Jesus and before the writing of the Gospels, those waiting for the 'Kingdom of Heaven' called 'hypocritical' those who were more realistic than they, and who knew how to combine acceptance of this world's time with an intrinsically religious spirit.[21]

Does this mean that relations between Jesus and the Pharisees were totally serene and peaceful and that polemics started only with the disciples? No, certainly not.[22] But a straightforward reading of the Gospels gives no clue to the extent to which the Pharisee movement constituted a spiritual renewal within Judaism. Jesus shared their views on many points. It has always been thought that the dedication of the Pharisees to the interpretation of the Law ended up stifling people by enclosing them within a straitjacket of impractical obligations. In reality, the Pharisees aimed to humanize the Law and make it applicable by taking concrete situations into account. And on more than one point where Jesus put himself in opposition to them, it is because he was free enough to push to the limit the application of one of their great principles, which was that the Law cannot

---

[21] Schubert, *Jésus*, pp. 44–5.
[22] Schubert, *Jésus*, pp. 62–9 and 119–33.

be directed against the vital interests of persons.[23] As to their 'mercenary' conception of relations with God, let it suffice to open the first page of the Sayings of the Fathers: 'Be not like servants who serve the master for condition of receiving a gift, but be like servants, who serve the master not on condition of receiving a gift.'[24] And if the Gospels constantly bring the Pharisees onto the scene, one is inclined to think that it is chiefly because they liked to be with Jesus to contrast their own teachings with his.

However, there are no suggestions of any of this in the commentaries we have been quoting; on the contrary, they go beyond the words of the Evangelists in order to accentuate the typical nature of the characters. Thus, according to our authors, in the trial and judgement of Christ 'the Pharisees were revenged for their pride that had been wounded by Jesus'.[25] Yet, if the Pharisees are presented throughout the Gospels as the chief adversaries of Jesus, in fact, they disappear before his arrest. The accounts of the Passion, the shaping of which is earlier than that of the remainder of the Gospels, are nearer to historical truth in the modern sense of the word. In accounts whose redaction came later the Pharisees tend to personify a more and more conventional type.

The discourse of which we have just been reading a few examples verges even more on caricature and goes even further than the Evangelists in taking liberties with history. But can we use and misuse terms such as 'Law, Jew, Judaism' as if they applied merely to fictitious and purely symbolic types, when in fact they primarily refer to people and institutions that are always likely to be assimilated to these conventional archetypes?

[23] Schubert, *Jésus,* pp. 55–8 and 65–6.

[24] *Mishna Aboth,* 1.3. *Pirke Aboth. The Ethics of the Talmud: Sayings of the Fathers* (text, complete translation and commentaries by R. Travers Herford; New York: Schocken, 1962), p. 23.

[25] Emmaus Sunday Missal, p. 237.

Preaching

New Testament texts referring to the Jews cannot therefore be read in a naive manner and ecclesiastical documents give frequent reminders that readings must be accompanied by explanations and appropriate commentaries.[26]

Unfortunately, as noted by K. Hruby, 'the traditional opposition between Judaism and Christianity clearly offers ideal opportunities for facile rhetoric'.[27] Consider the following on the star of the wise men:

> This star shines throughout their journey of faith except at Jerusalem. Jerusalem is the only city without a star ... While the Gentile cities see the 'Morning Star' shine above them (The Revelation to John 2.28; 22.16), Jerusalem has extinguished her stars and prefers darkness to light, her ancient parchments to the Word become Flesh. Leaders, scribes and priests who should have been the watchers of the night, the first to see the rising of the 'star emerging from Jacob' (Numbers 24.17) have fallen asleep over the scrolls of the prophets. Lost in their scrutiny of the letter, they have missed the Star.[28]

And here again is the inevitable charge against the Pharisees:

> The Pharisees are those ultras who take themselves for God's detectives and spend their lives distributing fines for the least infringement of their rules.[29]

The same police analogy illustrates the manner in which Jesus fulfils the Law:

---

[26] Guidelines and Suggestions for Implementing the Conciliar Declaration *Nostra Aetate* no. 4, January 1975, in Croner (ed.), *Stepping Stones*, p. 11. See also the remarks of Cardinal Willebrands to the Roman Synod of 1977.

[27] Hruby, *Les Relations entre le judaïsme et l'Eglise*, p. 32.

[28] Amédée Brunot, *Homilies for Year A: Sundays and Feast Days* (Mulhouse: Salvator, 1977), p. 47.

[29] Brunot, *Homilies for Year A*, p. 148.

by returning the Law to the original simplicity that Scribes and Pharisees had buried beneath the jumble of their desiccating casuistry ... Jesus, in contrast to the Jewish moralists, does not stay on the surface of the law to multiply its complications and prohibitions.[30]

Entitled 'The appeal to the exploited'; here is a description of Jesus' audience:

His audience consists of humble people often crushed by the weight of their daily toil and despised by their religious leaders who weigh them down under the yoke of the Talmud, a code of prescriptions impossible to observe, always exploited by masters whose only scruples are liturgical.[31]

These unscrupulous masters 'have transformed the Torah into the Talmud, that is to say they have abandoned an ever-living attachment to the living God for the sake of a roll of parchment covered with prescriptions and interdicts'.[32]

We also hear that 'the destruction of Jerusalem ... was the official seal of the passing from the old to the new covenant'.[33]

The better to illustrate his subject, the author invites us to observe present-day Jews praying in order to see a living demonstration of what Jesus stigmatized:

It is worth reading the gospel condemnation (Matthew 23. 1–12) in front of the Wailing Wall or in a synagogue of Mea Shearim in Jerusalem in order to understand it. We can then grasp the distinction between justice according to the Law and the justice of faith, between the sclerotic and the new covenant, between the ministry of the letter and that of the spirit, between speech and action, between respect for a dated past and attention to this present life, between men

---

[30] Brunot, *Homilies for Year A*, pp. 132–3.
[31] Brunot, *Homilies for Year A*, p. 162.
[32] Brunot, *Homilies for Year A*, p. 204.
[33] Brunot, *Homilies for Year A*, p. 211.

turning their backs to the crowd and those who make themselves small in the midst of the crowd. Following Jesus, Matthew refuses to have a Christian rabbinate in the Church.[34]

It is true that the same author introduces his commentary on the Gospel according to St Mark with a beautiful evocation of the hope of Israel. But in a new edition, he returns to the so-called Wailing Wall to renew his thoughts on pharisaic piety:

> Talmudic Jews ... flounce about groaning, venting their religious and national passion with theatrical gestures. While I gaze at the sons of the Pharisees before the Wailing Wall, a word much loved by Paul VI comes back to me: coherence. Living in the midst of these wailers, Jesus tapped into the inspiration of the prophets ... to diagnose this pharisaic malady: incoherence coupled with a ridiculous vanity: 'They talk and do nothing'. They seek to dominate, to parade themselves, to preside and give themselves titles! Are the stinging remarks of Jesus out of date? Isn't pharisaism the permanent temptation of every Church?[35]

Here we see at work one of the moving forces behind this perfunctory contrast between Judaism and Christianity: the fact of considering Judaism as a negative reference point which enables the Christian to identify the risk against which he must protect himself. As if to insinuate that what is specifically Jewish could accidentally become Christian. There are theology courses, for example, that explain that the Church must beware of the 'Judaic' temptation.

---

[34] Brunot, *Homilies for Year A*, p. 222.
[35] Amédée Brunot, *New homilies for Year A*, in French (Mulhouse: Salvator, 1980), pp. 236–7.

Theology

Theology itself is not above playing this tune in order to make the originality of the gospel clearer. Consider, for example, this account of the way Jesus is said to have conceived his own relation to the Mosaic Law: 'He wanted to redefine the relationship between Israel and God – in complete discontinuity with the Law and without taking the tradition of the masters or the authority of the priests into account.[36]

But what is the Law? Though the term is used again and again throughout the work, it is never defined. We learn that 'the Law came from Moses, or at least, the authority of Moses guaranteed its validity' (p. 72). It constitutes the foundation of a power and an institution that Jesus came to dismantle (pp. 72–3) and is embodied in a series of 'observances' whose 'divine origin' Jesus contested by denouncing the 'stupidity of petty legalism' (pp. 32–3). In short, in the time of Jesus Mosaic Law seems to be no more than an alienating legalism totally foreign to the spirit of Scripture, something that Jesus attacks as an outsider. What indeed is there in common between Jesus and Judaism? 'His teaching does not refer to the tradition of the elders but he consciously presents himself as an antithesis' (p. 69).

Besides, the God of Jesus is not that of the 'Establishment': 'The liberties that Jesus takes with the Law and with worship demonstrate that he does not simply preach a conversion acceptable within the limits of Judaism but introduces a principle that nullifies the way in which Judaism had organized its relationship with God. The God of Jesus is not the God of the official religion' (p. 73).

Jesus is thus not in any way indebted to 'the guarantors of religious orthodoxy and the true Jewish tradition' (p. 76). Naturally, he 'is unafraid of associating with them but he

---

[36] Duquoc, *Jésus, homme libre*, p. 76. This work has been re-edited regularly since it first appeared.

regards their authority as worthless'.[37] This is because they have claimed excessive power for themselves:

> Pharisees, scribes and Sadducees are attacked as the dominating classes possessing an unwarranted power to interpret the Law. Jesus condemns their social function; it is their power he wants to break, and in this he witnesses to his freedom. His rebellion against the masters of the Law is a rebellion on behalf of the little ones on whom their masters impose an unbearable yoke. They do not know that God gives freedom. They impose their social conventions and their rules on God. Jesus gives God back his liberty by defying the power of the scribes and Pharisees and by refusing to acknowledge the validity of their 'authority' (p. 30).

The death of Jesus is thus an ineluctable consequence of his opposition to the religious authorities and signifies 'the triumph of the Pharisees' way of searching for God' (p. 85).

Sadducean doctors of the Law, Pharisees and Sadducees are together in the same boat, weighing the people down by a common oppression; the relation of Jesus to the Pharisees is defined in terms of class warfare; the death of Jesus is presented as a victory of the Pharisees ... Concern for historical rigour, affirmed several times in the course of the work, seems to evaporate as soon as Jewish institutions are mentioned, at which point the whole tone of the discourse changes and characters and institutions are reduced to the level of mere symbols.

Critical Reflection

It must be made clear that even if the texts cited form, by their very connection, a rather dismaying collection, we must not assume that they are representative of present-day Christian

---

[37] Duquoc, *Jésus, homme libre*, p. 29. Such an affirmation is hard to reconcile with Matt. 23.3.

teaching on Judaism. A survey of theological texts would certainly demonstrate a much more subtle approach. Christology is well aware that Jesus is situated within a tradition and systematic recourse to perfunctory contrasts is usually avoided in liturgical literature.

Having said that, the examples we have cited cannot be disregarded, though they represent merely a marginal and insignificant stream of thought. They were taken mainly – on purpose – from literature without any scholarly pretensions and that does not purport to be giving an account of Judaism in itself; as such they are all the more representative of a type of discourse that does not trouble to justify statements assumed to be undeniable. Besides, the mere fact that these texts are widely distributed shows that such language is considered perfectly acceptable.

To present Judaism in this way is not only unjust to Judaism, it actually threatens to impoverish and distort Christianity itself.

A Distorted Version of Judaism

The Judaism portrayed in the citations above has only the loosest of connections with historical reality. A Judaism of this kind would have no continuity either with what went before or with what came immediately afterwards.

Cut off from its past: there is surely a certain incoherence in a course of liturgical readings that take us through a spiritual deepening in the biblical tradition whose final pages lead to 'the threshold of the New Testament', only to present us a mere few years after *Wisdom* with a 'late Judaism' that looks like nothing more than a desiccated legalism.

Cut off from what followed as well: how could this barren tree have flowered into the spiritual tradition that sustains present-day Judaism, the richness of which the texts we have just read give not a hint? Nothing in these descriptions offers us the faintest notion that Judaism might be worth knowing; one wonders what could possibly be the object and content of the 'loyal dialogue'[38] that one of our authors would love to be able to undertake with the Jewish people.

But is it really historical Judaism that these texts are talking about?

In all the citations above, Judaism appears only in order to highlight the contrast with the person of Jesus and the newness of his message. There is a desire to demonstrate that this newness is permanent, that Jesus is the same today as he was yesterday, that he never ceases to denounce injustice and to liberate people from all that stops them from living. The person of Jesus must stand out against a background in which priority is given to elements that seem to have a universal significance in time and space. We do not even notice how Judaism is then simply brought onto the scene to be equated with whatever Jesus came to fight against; it becomes a symbol of slavery and even of the death from which the resurrection of Jesus came to save us. One of our authors has no hesitation in writing that for the 'religious person' of the time of Jesus, 'the honour of God', which is the 'aim of the Law and of religion', leads directly to 'contempt for humanity' and 'results in homicide'.[39]

Another, after a very beautiful description of the mystical significance of the Sabbath, affirms that in codifying it, the Pharisees turned it into a symbol of servitude. He ends by defining the mutual relations between the Sabbath, the Pharisees and Jesus himself thus: 'To those who transformed people into robots and mummies by such minutiae, he came to say "Untie him and let him go".'[40] 'The Sabbath of the Pharisees will get the better of Jesus, at least for twenty-four hours. Jesus lies in a grave throughout the whole of a Sabbath.'[41]

When Judaism is reduced to a few negative abstractions to

---

[38] Brunot, *Homilies for Year A*, p. 182.

[39] Cf. *supra*, pp. 15–16.

[40] A. Brunot, *Homilies for Year B: Sundays and Feastdays* (Mulhouse: Salvator, 1978), p. 180.

[41] Brunot, *Homilies for Year B,* p. 151.

which a universal significance is attributed, what is that but the creation of nothing less than a myth?

In any case, is the result as universal as it seems? It is all too clear that this discourse reflects the sensibilities of a given epoch. At the beginning of the twentieth century preaching did not turn Pharisees into figures of 'Power' or of the 'Establishment', nor was Judaism regarded as a symbol of 'religion' in contrast to pure Christian faith. Anti-Judaism does seem to have the virtue, while remaining true to itself, of reflecting the sensibilities of the time.

A Mutilated Christianity

Unjust to Judaism as it is, this vision is inadequate to account for the place of Jesus in the history of salvation.

First of all, it is fair to wonder how this manner of situating Christ in relation to the Judaism of his time can account for the formation of the spiritual personality of Jesus. By what subterranean path could the spiritual tradition of the Old Testament have disappeared as the Christian era drew near, only to make a mysterious return to life in Christ and then in the Church? In what way is Jesus the tributary of the milieu in which he grew? And if he owes nothing to this milieu, then how can his humanity be taken seriously? No doubt his conduct was motivated by nothing other than 'his filial attitude toward God and the strength of his love for his neighbour'.[42] But was his relationship to his Father and to other people somehow divorced from his assimilation of the Torah, a Law of holiness received within a living tradition? Was the relation of Jesus to his Father something separate from and parallel with Jewish faith and piety?

To situate Jesus in relation to his people, it is not enough to stress his condemnation of religious formalism.

No one could seriously doubt the fact that Jesus vigorously

---

[42] Duquoc, *Jésus, homme libre*, pp. 33–4.

lambasted the formality of some ostentatiously pious Pharisees and of religion diverted away from its true spirit. Here it was not just to the prophets he was heir: Jewish tradition itself includes criticisms parallel to those brought us by the Gospels and addressed to bad Pharisees. Nor will anyone deny that religious groups are all liable to such deviations which are not, therefore, specifically Jewish. Besides, Christian preaching would not attack 'Pharisaism' with such vigour, were it not to be identifiable within the Church herself. There is food for thought in our attempts to identify in other people's behaviour what we are not keen to face up to in ourselves.

Jesus was, without a doubt, quite conscious of the dangers he exposed himself to by his freedom of speech, action and judgement when facing the religious authorities of his time. But that does not help us to understand in what consisted his awareness of being more than a prophet.

The central point here is his relationship to the Law, provided that this term is understood not in its restricted sense of a legal code but in its proper significance of Torah: the drama played out around Jesus concerns his awareness of his relation to the Word of God and to God himself. Nothing authorizes us to think that Jesus was not a good Jew, faithful to the letter and the spirit of the legal observances. And if he allowed himself to perform healings on the Sabbath, it was not in the name of plain old 'common sense' as opposed to 'the stupidity of legal small-mindedness' or because of a supposedly relatively lax attitude that Galileans had toward Judaism. It was because he was aware that, in him, the kingdom had come and that, in him, the Torah had reached its culmination. Far from opposing the Torah, Jesus consciously identified with it. It was on this very basis that he offered himself as an object of faith; it was on this basis that he was to be accepted or rejected. If we are to appreciate the ultimate implications of the act of faith, we cannot allow ourselves to underestimate the unprecedented nature of a claim of this sort made by a mortal, whatever the manner in which he expressed his awareness of himself. The opposition that Jesus, and then his disciples, encountered from

within Judaism was not dictated by petty-mindedness: present-
ing this opposition in such a way as to arouse facile indignation
runs the risk of reducing faith to mere good faith. None of the
authors quoted would agree with so extreme a conclusion but it
is unfortunate that some of the expressions they use carry the
risk of being reduced to such an interpretation.

✡ ✡ ✡

It must be stressed that the few examples examined must not be
in any way considered as providing a summary of contemporary
Christian teaching on Judaism. But they are witnesses to the
Church's persisting tendency to define Christian identity over
against Judaism.

This polarity springs from the New Testament. The first
Christians who came from Judaism progressively affirmed their
identity in expressing what distinguished them from other Jews:
the fact of having recognized in Jesus of Nazareth the Messiah
of Israel. The New Testament is a witness to the trials through
which the young community progressively defined itself in
opposition to official Judaism. But the authors of the New
Testament would not have blamed 'the Jews', the Pharisees and
the synagogue with so much vigour, had they not been aware of
being authentic Israelites themselves.

Today's Christian coming from the Gentiles must remain
conscious of the fact that his situation is not that of Paul or of
Matthew. Can he accept the polemical material in the New
Testament, his heritage, without a minimum of hermeneutic,
when the expression of his own identity itself requires stressing
all that unites him to the trunk onto which he has been grafted?

7

A Christian Identity in Communion with Israel

Defining the Christian condition by contrasting it system-atically with Judaism is therefore a habit that seems to have solid roots in the Christian mentality. Such an attitude, unfair to Judaism that finds itself redefined and caricatured according to an idealized picture of Christianity, ends up impoverishing and distorting the Christian faith itself.

Hence, it is necessary to show that the Christian identity involves a reference to and even a communion with the people of Israel.

'As this sacred Synod searches into the mystery of the Church, it recalls the spiritual bond linking the people of the New Covenant with Abraham's stock.'[1] In this manner, perhaps not even deliberately, the Council demonstrated the paradox of the reciprocal situation of the Church and of the Jewish people. The Council considered Judaism in a document dealing with the non-Christian religions, but by searching into her own mystery, the Christian Church acknowledges her spiritual communion with Abraham's stock. The Church cannot speak of the Jewish people as of some foreign body. We shall return to this double relation of interiority and exteriority, which in fact constitutes a thread guiding reflection on the links between the Church and the Jewish people. Let us now turn and 'search into the mystery of the Church' to

---

[1] *Nostra Aetate* no. 4.

remind ourselves, at least in outline, of what it is that Christianity receives from its Jewish source.

Jesus

Acknowledgement of what Christianity receives from Israel needs to begin with the person of Jesus of Nazareth.

Jesus is Jewish. Is it certain that Christian reflection has always given enough attention to the implications of this statement?

When Christology attempts to get to grips with the human and spiritual personality of Jesus, it naturally starts with the words and actions of the Nazarene. By examining the testimony of the Gospels, it tries to understand who the man was, what is revealed by his words and gestures, and what awareness he had of himself and of his relations with God. In a study of this sort, theology concentrates almost exclusively on the period between the baptism by John the Baptist and the death on the cross, as if the whole of Jesus were to be found in what we are told about his public life. Apart from generalities on the humanity of Jesus, the preceding period most often only provides matter for more or less pious considerations on the carpenter's life in the workshop in Nazareth. In other words, all too often the assumption is made that the time when Jesus had something to say was the only meaningful phase in his life, while the time when he was silent is insignificant.

In saying this, there can be no question of getting involved in a risky attempt to reconstitute the years of his hidden life. But what is needed is to take seriously the fact that during these years Jesus, 'born of a woman, born a subject of the Law' (Gal. 4.4), lived, thought, spoke, prayed as a Jew. Moreover, the Evangelists relate the astonishment of the inhabitants of Nazareth when Jesus returned to preach the gospel in his own country,[2] with the clear implication that until the time of

---

[2] Matt. 13.53–8, Mark 6.1–6; Luke 4.16–30.

his baptism, Jesus was indistinguishable from his fellow-citizens. No matter how interesting it is to consider the lowliness of the Son of God and his solidarity with the poor, the very first lesson to draw from his years in Nazareth is surely that Jesus was a child of Israel in the biblical sense of the word. Impossible though it is to penetrate the mystery of his consciousness, we are perfectly justified in stating that in the unity and the truth of his being he felt perfectly at home among the people of the Covenant. If he frequented the synagogue, it was because he felt he could make the prayer of Israel his own, expressing through it the relation which united him to his Father, unique though that relation was.

Today, theology has rediscovered the need to take Jesus' humanity seriously. This means recognizing that his humanity was constructed through a network of relationships, by use of a certain language, by assimilation of a culture, by ways of thinking, speaking, praying. Although it is important to take the decisive step of the baptism by John the Baptist with the utmost seriousness, it would be absurd to regard this step as a break with his previous life. Jesus is not a convert; his entry into public life under the action of the Holy Spirit cannot be regarded as a disavowal of his past life. This latter was taken up and integrated first into his public life and then into the resurrection through the power of the Father. Christian faith cannot deny that the coming of Jesus and the proclamation of the gospel constituted something radically new without being emptied of its content. But this newness is in no way to be understood as a sort of dialectical contradiction such as would turn Jesus into the antithesis of his origins. If the baptism does constitute a break, it is only in the way that a bud bursts forth under the pressure of the sap that brought it to life. In his reflections on prayer, Abraham Heschel says that the word can be no other than *le trop-plein du silence*[3] (i.e. 'the overflowing of

---

[3] From the French translation of Heschel's work. In English the text runs: 'Prayer is . . . the outpouring of the heart before Him.' A. Heschel, 'Prayer', *Review of Religion* (January 1945), pp. 153–68.

silence'). The word that resounded when Jesus entered into public life was the overflowing of a silence that had been nourished by the faith, the hope and the prayers of the people of Israel. It was among this people that Jesus became what he was.

Wanting to create a dichotomy between Judaism and Jesus means not only detaching Christ from what linked him to his past – which would dehumanize him – it also implies introducing a dichotomy within Christ himself. If the Jesus of public life is in contradiction with Judaism, he is in contradiction with his own past. Defining the relation of Christ to Judaism in terms of dichotomy and contradiction is ultimately to put a question mark over the unity of the very person of Jesus.

The Word

To say that Jesus is Jewish is not just a matter of defining a belongingness to a specific culture when the culture of the people concerned is the Word of God itself. The person of Jesus expresses the unity of a Word that is continually becoming flesh. It is the same Word that brings together a people, that becomes incarnate in Jesus, and that is displayed in the Church, the body of Christ.

When Moses, at the foot of Mt Sinai, 'took the Book of the Covenant, he read it to the listening people, who then said, "We shall do and we shall hear"' (Exod. 24.7). Jewish tradition took note of the paradox constituted by the order of words in the verse, which evokes the fact that the Word is done before it is heard, underlining that the Word of God cannot be heard if it is not done, that is to say, accomplished by practice. Here again, we must recognize that certain routine preconceptions too often prevent the Christian from acquiring a sufficiently deep understanding of what is involved. Even though exegesis realized a long time ago that the word 'Torah' cannot adequately be translated by the modern word 'Law',[4] Christian discourse all too often continues to reduce the practice of the Mosaic Law to the minutiae of observances, and Judaism itself to soulless legalism.[5] We are very far from terms used in Scripture itself for which the Torah is the Way, Truth and Life.[6]

The Word of God cannot be heard without being put into practice. It is the code of the Covenant that creates a people and gives it structure. It is a rule of life which transforms man so as to make him righteous. The Word becomes literally incarnate as soon as a person allows himself to be fashioned by it. As an expression of the holiness of God, it brings to rebirth in the image of his Creator whoever welcomes and assimilates it, making that person holy as God is holy (Lev. 19.2, cf. Matt. 5.48).

This is the unique Word which Christian faith affirms to be incarnate in Jesus Christ.

When the Epistle to the Hebrews quotes Psalm 40 to apply it to Christ, it says with the Greek Bible: 'You gave me a body' (Heb. 10.5). The Hebrew original says: 'You gave me an open ear' (Ps. 40.6). Whatever were the reasons of the translators, the variant is not without meaning. The ancients apparently thought that the formation of the human body starts with the ear, so the whole being is thus embodied in the capacity to hear the word. Within a people, the existence of which depends on accepting the invitation: 'Hear, oh Israel!' the humanity of Jesus is born from the coming of the Word into a being of flesh and blood.

Without wishing to repeat the entire content of Christian faith about the incarnate Word, it is necessary to observe that the incarnation is part of a coherence and a continuity. The

---

[4] The word 'Torah' comes from a verb which means *shooting an arrow* or *indicating a direction.*

[5] A good number of the criticisms that the Gospels address to certain categories of Pharisees are to be found in virtually identical form in that monument of pharisaic literature, the Talmud (see for example *B. Sota* 22b).

[6] See for example Ps. 119.3, 17, 142, etc.

Christian who confesses, with the Gospel of John, that 'the Word became flesh' (John 1.14), should not of course attempt to belittle the unique and unprecedented manner in which the Word of God in Jesus Christ became personally united to a human nature. The Christian must understand respectfully that it is impossible for a Jew to accept the Christian conception of the incarnation. But unless the Christian is going to cast doubt on the actual oneness of God, he must recognize in Jesus the person in whom the One Word of the One God takes flesh. Jesus, in whom God recapitulates that which he says of himself to humanity, is the righteous person who coincides perfectly with the Torah. Reflection on the relationship between Jesus and the Mosaic Law must begin before all else by recognizing in Christ the one in whom the Word given to Israel takes flesh.

Finally, it is the same Word that we see at work giving birth to a Church[7] that sees herself as the Body of Christ. In the Church, the Gentiles, who 'have heard the message of the truth' (Eph. 1.13) are brought into communion with the chosen people and 'have the same inheritance and form the same body and enjoy the same promise in Christ Jesus through the Gospel' (Eph. 3.6).

Scripture

That is why the Church reads the Scriptures, acknowledging that it is 'today' (Luke 4.21) that they are fulfilled.

Here, we need to observe that the New Testament does not claim to be sufficient unto itself, for its whole meaning arises from its reference to a Scripture to which it constantly refers and which it comes to interpret. It does not come as a substitute for an *Old* Testament thereby suddenly made obsolete. Nor does it come as an addition to the Old Testament to complete it. And the Church, in accepting the New Testament, is not

---

[7] Acts 6.7; 12.24; 13.49; 19.20, etc.

entitled to consider herself exempted from reading the Law and the Prophets, for the New Testament affirms that the Law and the Prophets only yield the plenitude of their meaning in the resurrection of Jesus.

This truth is evidenced so massively in the New Testament itself, that we can only set it out in outline here, even as we marvel at how often it is neglected in practice. The resurrected Jesus explains from Scripture everything that concerns him (Luke 24.27) and the first Christian sermon proclaims that the prophecies have been fulfilled (Acts 2.14–36). When the first Christian communities read the Scriptures, they were clearly reading what we call the Old Testament, and the gospels, progressively put down in writing, are witness to the manner in which Christian faith re-read the Law and the Prophets in the light of the resurrection. The New Testament cannot be regarded as an autonomous text; it presents as a key to the reading of the Scriptures. The key cannot be self-sufficient, nor can it be substituted for what it comes to open.

That is why we may justifiably ask whether the New Testament can even properly be called Scripture.[8] Without wishing to take part in this debate, it is worth noting that mainstream Christian tradition does not put the Bible and the Gospels on the same level. The New Testament does not come simply to lengthen the list of the 'holy books'. And the well-known saying of St Augustine, whereby the 'New is hidden inside the Old, and the Old is revealed in the New'[9] attests to the fact that the two 'testaments' refer to each other and that each, therefore, is unique of its kind. The resurrected Jesus opens the minds of his disciples to an understanding of

---

[8] Without omitting the fact that the Second Epistle of Peter includes the letters of Paul as a part of Scripture (2 Pet. 3.16), F. Rossi de Gasperis calls the New Testament a Christian 'midrash', an expression he borrowed from R. Gordis (Rossi de Gasperis, 'Israele', p. 125 and n. 54).

[9] The formula is repeated by Vatican II. Cf. Constitution *Dei Verbum*, chap. 4, no. 16. For reflections on the unity of the two testaments, see the books of P. Beauchamp, *L'Un et l'Autre Testament* (Paris: Seuil, 1976), and *Le Récit, la Lettre et le Corps* (Paris: Cerf, 1982).

the Scriptures and these, in return, witness to the identity of Jesus.

In the end, experience shows that Christian preaching soon runs out of breath if it limits itself to commenting on apostolic writings in which the vocabulary appears to owe nothing to the Old Testament. It can even fall into aberration, or at least impoverish if not mutilate the expression of Christian faith, if it allows itself to ignore the scriptural content of the expressions it uses, or to pass over certain fundamental categories of biblical revelation which permeate the New Testament. If these are ignored, we are left with some huge insoluble problems in the New Testament itself. Let us think of such fundamental concepts as Covenant, promise, people, redemption, not forgetting such terms as Scripture and fulfilment, all of them terms hard to ignore in the New Testament.

This is yet another area where recent history gives us an example of an entirely new situation that the Christian must welcome with gratitude as well as with humility: the discovery by an increasing number of Christians of Jewish literature, contemporaneous with early Christian preaching, which brings renewed understanding of the Gospels and even of the person of Jesus. 'It is already evident that this Jesus of Nazareth, whom Christians believe they know so well, will be further revealed to them as he really was when the Jews have taught them to know him better'.[10] In this domain too, the Christian receiving the key to his own 'Scriptures' from the Jew, is protected from any temptation to complacency.

Old and New

Here, an objection will unfailingly be raised: attracting too much attention to links of continuity uniting the Jewish and Christian faiths surely means underestimating the extent to

---

[10] Bernard Dupuy, in his preface to the French translation of *Jesus* by David Flusser (Paris: Seuil, 1970), p. 19.

which the New Testament presents as *new*. Does it not imply forgetting all that Christianity contains as reinterpretation when it took over the Scriptures of Israel? Does it not also overestimate the common heritage? Is it not taking the risk of maintaining and fostering misunderstandings, opening the door to regrettable disappointments in inter-confessional dialogue.

The question is too vast to be treated here but too important to pass by. Even the briefest of answers will have to allow for careful distinctions.

It must first be remembered that the originality of Christianity is linked to the actual person of Jesus Christ. A full understanding of Christianity cannot consider him to be simply a Pharisee,[11] an Essene or a representative of one of the spiritual currents of the Judaism of his time. Affirmation of the divinity of Jesus, apparently irreconcilable with the transcendence of God even when situated as above within the continuity of biblical revelation, introduces between the Jew and the Christian a disagreement which must be acknowledged and accepted.

Attempting to reduce the uniqueness of the person of Jesus also weakens the central importance of his death and resurrection. If Jesus was not a more or less dissident prophet of Judaism who came to preach a new religion, Christianity was born from an act of faith, which recognizes in the life, death and resurrection of this man the event in which the salvation of the world is accomplished. This proposition regarding the actual person of Jesus, and not simply regarding the message he bears, is constitutive of Christian identity.

Having said that, an emphasis on the importance that adherence to the actual person of Jesus Christ has for the Christian, should not lead to a hardening of the classical opposition concerning the relative importance of faith and

---

[11] Christians may be surprised that Jesus could be regarded as a Pharisee. Let us recall that a straightforward reading of the Gospels does not show how the pharisaic movement constituted a renewal of Judaism and how its moral and spiritual teachings were close to those of the New Testament.

works. Neither should be reduced to a caricature of itself and we must avoid reasoning as if we were talking about two mutually exclusive conceptions. The Christian, who recognizes in the Passover of Jesus the salvific event to which he must assent through faith, knows that the new life given him must be demonstrated by the fruits of conversion. The Jew, for whom the restoration of the created world will come about through the fulfilment of the Torah, welcomes the Torah itself as a gift from God. The Christian knows that 'faith without works is useless' (Jas. 2.20) and the Jew cannot forget that 'the upright will live through faithfulness'.[12] On this point, as on all others, the Jewish and Christian faiths are open to each other; both Jew and Christian can always find, each within his own spiritual tradition, the specific elements by which the other defines himself.

Finally, we are very much in danger of going astray if we think we can find the originality of Christianity in the domain of moral and spiritual ideals. Neither love of one's neighbour nor of one's enemies, nor hope of salvation for all the nations, nor the idea of the fatherhood of God,[13] nor even the affirmation that man is not made for the Sabbath[14] is specific to Christianity. Here again, it cannot be too strongly emphasized that the Christian faith is connected to Judaism in terms of fulfilment and that it recognizes in Jesus the one who represents in his person the ultimate aspiration of the Torah itself. The prophets know that they are sinners and that they do not conform entirely to the message they bear. In Jesus, Christian faith recognizes the one who coincides perfectly with the Word and with the ideal of holiness that it expresses (cf. John 8.46). We may justifiably wonder how Jesus deepened the

---

[12] Hab. 2.4. Cf. *B. Maccoth* 24a which summarizes all the commandments in this verse of Habakkuk.

[13] For this point, to be approached with the utmost subtlety, see for example Flusser, *Jesus*, (Jerusalem: The Magnes Press, 1977), p. 186.

[14] 'The Sabbath has been given you, not you to the Sabbath' (*Mekhilta of Rabbi Ishmael on Exodus* 31.14).

law of love. But from the fact that Jesus brought the love of God and of his neighbour to their utmost perfection, it would be naive to conclude that Christians are better than Jews. Such a way of appropriating Christ runs clean contrary to faith; Christians cannot disregard their own inadequacies in respect of the law of charity by which they claim to define themselves. It is not possible merely to invoke the 'new commandment' as a way of defining the novelty of Christianity without at the same time asking ourselves how this ideal of charity has really expressed itself in history; that is to say without taking into account how it has been put into practice by those who claim to follow it. Besides, it would be inconsistent to declare that the gospel comes to liberate us from a law, the practice of which is above human powers, while affirming that Christianity is superior to Israel's religion because its moral demands are higher.

Above all, it must be remembered that the novelty brought by Christ appears within the chosen people. The Church, originally composed of Jews only, understood and defined itself as the *remnant* of Israel.[15] It was onto this remnant that the branches coming from paganism came to be grafted. The Church perceived and defined herself, not as a new Israel that would take the place of the old, but as an Israel renewed by the faithfulness of God to his one covenant. The idea of a first covenant with Israel supplanted by a second covenant with the Gentiles is foreign to the New Testament perspectives.

In historical terms, the gap widened between the Jewish people and a Church from which the Judaeo-Christian stream had disappeared. In parallel, within the Christian mentality the contrast hardened between a former order, to which Israel was witness, and a new order embodied in a Church become totally exterior to Israel. The *de facto* exteriority of the Church to the Jewish people, and vice versa, gave implicit reinforcement to the idea that the categories of the new and the old were themselves exterior to each other. The passage from the old to

---

[15] Cf. *infra*, p. 125 n. 2.

the new could be made only in terms of chronological succession visibly expressed by the replacement of the synagogue by the Church. Judaism became simply what had existed before Jesus Christ.

This is a far cry from the perspective of Scripture, for which the entirety of revelation reverberates with an ongoing movement from the old to the new. The Old Testament gives us a certain number of examples of renewals of the Covenant[16] while the New Testament invites the person already born in Christ to be renewed[17] and to learn from the past.[18] Affirmation of the decisive character of the renewal that was accomplished by the resurrection of Jesus and the sending of the Holy Spirit, must not prevent us from perceiving that this renewal, precisely because it is new, has deep roots within a certain continuity and a certain tradition. The very idea of a new covenant is an eminently Old Testament one,[19] and it is from Israel that the Church receives the very newness in terms of which she defines herself.

The dynamics of revelation are such that it cannot purely and simply be cut into two successive 'economies'. Separating the old from the new to make two 'religions' means fossilizing them and betraying them both.[20]

It also means excluding from the Christian condition ideas of progression and conversion. This theme has already been broached here several times. It appears that one of the reasons why Christianity has such difficulty in relating correctly to the Jewish people has to do with the trouble it has in coming to terms with the existence of sin within its own heart. There is a well-known discourse, which stigmatizes as 'Old Testament' or

---

[16] Exod. 34; Josh. 24; 2 Kings 22–23; 2 Chron. 34; Neh. 9–10.

[17] 2 Cor. 4.16; Col. 3.10, etc.

[18] 1 Cor. 10.1–11.

[19] Jer. 31.31–4. Cf. Ezek. 36.26–7. Need it be recalled that the New Covenant of which Jeremiah spoke was concluded with the Houses of Israel and of Judah?

[20] It should be noted that the Old Testament becomes introduced into the New by means of the genealogies of Jesus (Matt. 1.1–17; Luke 3.23–38).

even Judaic the resistance which people and institutions feel to letting themselves be renewed by the Holy Spirit.

Gift and Mediation

Christianity is not an autonomous religion, if such an expression may be used, because it comes with a built-in double bond from which it cannot be freed without losing its nature: first, to Scripture to which the New Testament makes constant reference *proprio motu*; secondly, to the people of Israel with whom the Gentile-Christian finds himself in communion by faith in Christ. These two links are strictly interconnected; they demonstrate how the Church lives by a Word received through the mediation of the people chosen by God for himself.

The New Testament witnesses to the fact that this mediation is accomplished in Jesus. But Jesus cannot be dissociated from his people either in his person or in his mission. Experience shows that, without adhering to faith in Christ, Israel in large measure remains for us the interpreter of the Word.

It is in the election of Abraham (cf. Gen. 12.3) that all the families of the earth receive God's blessing. Some of the resistance that the Gentile-Christian opposes to that 'economy', and his desire to appropriate the blessing to himself while refusing the mediation of the people chosen by God, probably demonstrate in a measure impossible to determine, his tendency to turn Christianity into an autonomous religion. In the same measure, Jesus is thereby dejudaized and appropriated by a type of Christianity that claims to be self-sufficient. But the gospel is mutilated by the refusal to accept the Old Testament. To be indifferent to the people of Israel is to refuse the unity sealed by the death of Christ. Communion with Israel is inscribed within the core of Christian identity.

The beginning of the second paragraph of the third version of the document of Vatican II on the Jews reads: 'The Church of Christ recognises "with a grateful spirit" (*grato animo*) that the origin of her faith and of her election is already to be found, according to the plan of God's salvation, in Moses and the Prophets.'[21] For obscure reasons having very little to do with theology,[22] the expression of this gratitude has disappeared from the definitive text which limits itself to a recognition of the origins of faith and election in the patriarchs, Moses and the prophets. The omission may perhaps be more important than it seems and one may ask whether the Church came very close to making a statement that it will still have to make sooner or later in one way or other. The Church cannot say that she exists by grace and that everything she has is a gift without including in her thankfulness an expression of gratitude for the intermediary through whom these gifts came. 'Salvation comes from the Jews' (John 4.22). The Christian cannot give thanks for the saving Word without blessing God for his choice of the mediator through whom this Word came to him.

[21] Hoch and Dupuy (eds), *Les Eglises devant le judaïsme*, p. 328.
[22] Laurentin, *L'Eglise et les juifs*, pp. 30–2.

8

Self-awareness

Since the Christian identity involves communion with Israel, we shall try to define more precisely the relation of the Church today to a Jewish people which, as for itself, does not recognize the Messiahship of Jesus.

Evidence from the New Testament

No answer can be given to the question without first asking what the New Testament says about the situation of the Jews themselves. Even without any particular exegetical skills, it is easy enough to draw a few essential conclusions from chs. 9 to 11 of the Epistle to the Romans, on the understanding that the teaching of the New Testament on this subject goes far beyond this particular passage.

The Teaching of Romans 9–11: Terminology – A Multiplicity of Approaches

What is, according to Romans 9–11, the situation of Jews who have not accepted Christ? The answer is not simple. To designate Jews who have not accepted the gospel, Paul expresses himself in at least four different ways which, at first sight, appear hard to reconcile among themselves. These apparent contradictions point to the complexity of the subject and must act as checks against any tendency to draw hasty or unqualified conclusions from isolated passages.

The first way of talking about the subject is that found, for example, in the first verses of ch. 9: 'They are Israelites; it was they who were adopted as children, the glory was theirs and the covenants; to them were given the Law and the worship of God and the promises. To them belong the fathers . . . (Rom. 9.4–5).

Here Paul is speaking of the Jews in the plural: 'They are Israelites'. For him, therefore, these Jews are not identified with Israel as such. But they still continue to be defined with reference to the covenants and the patriarchs; nothing in the passage indicates that they were from then on to be stripped of their title as sons of Israel. In analogous fashion, later on Paul says, '*they* (plural) are still well loved for the sake of their ancestors' (Rom. 11.28), a way of affirming that they are not excluded from the blessing accorded to the descendants of Abraham. Even if in Paul's view, they are not identified with *Israel*, they are nevertheless *Israelites*.

This way of talking does not really fit in with what underlies the verses that immediately follow:

Not all born Israelites belong to Israel, and not all the descendants of Abraham count as his children, for
  Isaac is the one through whom
  your Name will be carried on.
That is, it is not by being children through physical descent that people become children of God; it is the children of the promise that are counted as the heirs (Rom. 9.6–8).

This passage by itself might lead us to conclude that for Paul, those Jews who reject Christ are no more than sons of the flesh of Abraham and are not even sons of God.

This conclusion which, as we shall see, is far from summarizing Paul's thoughts on the subject, fits dialectically into the logic of his reasoning. He means to demonstrate that God is supremely free and cannot be accused of being 'unjust' (Rom. 9.14). God's freedom to opt in favour of a part of Israel fits in with a continuous series of elections which Paul quotes from Scripture itself when he refers to the choice of Isaac and then of Jacob. The apparent failure of the Word of God constituted by the refusal of Israel to recognize in Jesus the object of her hope, leads Paul to make use of the biblical theme of the 'remnant' (Rom. 9.27; 11.5). It is in that part of the chosen people that has believed in Christ that the true Israel is concentrated. It is for that remnant that the Word of God is fulfilled and therefore it has not failed (9.6). Following this line of reasoning, the 'others' have excluded themselves from the blessings of the promise. They are no more than 'children according to the flesh'. Further on (11.17), Paul speaks of them as of branches that have been broken off, though he immediately corrects the irremediability of this image by evoking the possibility of the natural branches being grafted back onto their own trunk.

We would not be totally faithful to Paul's thinking if we dismissed this negative way of speaking about the Jews as purely methodological. However, it is surely the case that this way of speaking is only the necessary obverse of Paul's central affirmation in support of which it provides an argument *a contrario*: God is not unfaithful to his Word and the election of a remnant is the sign of his faithfulness.

The third way of referring to the Jews does not fit in with the two former ones, and especially not with the second; it consists of designating them simply and without any qualification by the term Israel.[1] In one case at least,[2] Paul opposes Israel, which 'did not succeed in fulfilling the Law', to the Gentiles who found 'the saving justice that comes of faith'. The 'remnant' has no place here where Paul talks as if faith in Christ were a matter for the Gentiles alone, and as if the faith of a few Jews were of no significance. The representative part of Israel, the part that conserves the name, is that which does not recognize the Messiahship of Jesus.

---

[1] Rom. 9.31; 10.19; 11.7.

[2] 9.31. If the *chosen* of 11.17 are the *remnant*, their mention attenuates the exclusivity of the preceding phrase ('Israel failed to find what it was seeking'). If it concerns believers coming from the Gentiles, their mention, on the other hand, reinforces the opposition between the Gentiles and Israel.

A fourth way of designating the Jews can be identified in the expression 'part of Israel'[3] which at once entails as its correlative reference to 'all Israel'.[4]

If the logic of each of these ways of designating the Jews is pushed to its limit, four different closed theological visions can be constructed, all four mutually exclusive. Designating by the term 'Israel' those Jews who do not adhere to faith in Christ, for instance, does not fit in with recognition of the 'remnant' as that part of the chosen people which continues as the elect and even less with the affirmation that 'not all born Israelites belong to Israel'. We face, therefore, a complex reality that cannot be expressed adequately by any single formula. Each manner of expression has to be weighed to see what it is saying; none must be given a privileged position so as to exclude the others.

The second approach, appealing to the theme of the remnant, may be taken as fairly representative of the manner in which Christian tradition has generally viewed the mutual relationship of the Church and the Jewish people.

In this type of expression what is first affirmed is the Church's awareness of her own spiritual identity: by recognizing in Jesus the fulfilment of the hope of Israel, the Church places herself squarely in the line of continuity of the promise and of the election. If she affirms that 'the Gentiles now have the same inheritance' (Eph. 3.6) it is because she sees in Jesus the one who can, by right, extend the blessing of the promise to the Gentiles. This proposition cannot be either weakened or overlooked without the Christian faith being emptied of its content.

As Paul recognized in Jesus the one in whom God fulfilled the promises made to Israel, he could not but consider it as a failure when a part of Israel refused to take the decisive step which would have allowed it to reach the object of its hopes. Today as yesterday, only God can determine the real content of

---

[3] 11.25. If that is the correct translation. It is the option taken by the NJB.
[4] Expression used by the NJB (Rom. 11.26).

that refusal, but this subjective aspect is not central to Paul's thought when he contrasts the 'children of the flesh' with the 'children of the promise'. In affirming 'Is it possible that they have not heard? Indeed they have...' (Rom. 10.18) Paul even seems to block the way to any recourse to a plea of ignorance. From a *situation* of refusal described so starkly, we must admit that it is always allowable to deduce a lesson of universal application already set out in the Law and the Prophets: any free human being has the liberty not to respond to an appeal made to him.

The account outlined above thus expresses truths there is no point in hiding, but it is insufficient to define the respective situations of Jews and Christians. It cannot be taken to its logical extreme without doing violence to other aspects of reality no less essential and affirmed just as strongly in the same passage. When Paul speaks of 'branches broken off through their unbelief' (11.20), he wants to warn the Gentile-Christian against making the same mistake. To *identify* Jews by their rejection of Christ and all that Christ represents is, as we have seen, to refuse to hear the lesson and to deny that the Church too is capable of being unfaithful to Christ. To reduce Jews after the coming of Christ to 'children of the flesh', as Christian teaching has done so often since the time of the Fathers of the Church, is to make nothing of the statements at the beginning of Romans 9 and to lock ourselves into an oversimplification whose limitations were demonstrated by Paul himself. To make the Church purely and simply the universal heir of Abraham means to forget that Paul himself mentions the existence of a 'part of Israel' without which we cannot speak of 'all Israel'.

The third way of talking, whereby Paul draws a simple contrast between 'Israel' and 'the Gentiles' underlines the paradox constituted by the fact that Gentiles have obtained what was the hope of Israel. This contrast between Gentile nations who came to faith and an Israel that remained overwhelmingly exterior to the gospel, represents an actual situation not without theological significance. It reveals – and we shall come back to this later – that even after Christ, Israel and the Gentiles remain exterior to each other. But it does not take into account the fact that the Jewish presence, modest and ambiguous[5] though it may be, has never completely disappeared from the Church. Neither does it express the bond of continuity that unites the Church to Israel through that part of the chosen people who received Christ and onto whom were grafted the branches which came from the Gentiles. A theology of the relations between the Church and the Jewish people based only on a vision of the duality Israel–Gentiles could define the relation only in terms of replacement. To an Israel henceforth deprived of its privileges would succeed a Church of the Gentiles, which would define herself purely and simply as a 'new Israel' by appropriating the unclaimed inheritance to herself.

In their diversity and even in their apparent contradictions, the different discourses interwoven in Romans 9–11 suggest a reality which is far too complex to be expressed in simple propositions, and this is what we must now try to approach.

It is a historical fact that certain Jews have indeed welcomed the gospel while the greater part of Israel has refused to recognize Jesus of Nazareth as the Messiah. In this sense, the proclamation of the gospel has caused a division within the Jewish people. This is perhaps what is meant by the sword of which Simeon speaks (Luke 2.35). But this analysis must not blind us to another observation, perhaps a deeper one, which definitely seems to be authorized by the passage in Romans just examined.

By stating that 'it is the children of the promise that are counted as the heirs' (Rom. 9.8), Paul shows first of all that, for him, the spiritual identity of the chosen people is clearly concentrated in those Jews who have accepted Christ. And in designating as 'children of physical descent' (9.8) those who have not made this act of faith, he does no more than repeat in a negative form, what is the principal object of his proposition

---

[5] Ambiguous because the 'natural' branches appear as if grafted onto a trunk that is in fact foreign to them from the *cultural* point of view.

and what constitutes its cutting edge, namely, that the Jewish people that believe in Christ *is* Israel.

But when he contrasts the Gentiles who have welcomed the gospel with an Israel that remains exterior to faith in Christ, though without losing its name, he affirms at one and the same time that the Jewish people that did not accept the gospel *is* Israel.

Here are two propositions which must both be accepted, and which we must be careful not to weaken for the sake of a facile or superficial harmony. We are confronted here by a reality much deeper than that expressed by the mere statement that one part of Israel believed in Christ and the other did not.

The reality of the chosen people is to be found in the 'remnant' that will receive the believers from the Gentiles to form the Church. But the Jewish people who did not accept Christ and who remained faithful to Judaism do not any the less keep, as a people, the spiritual identity conferred on them by the Covenant. If the term 'mystery' is defined as 'spiritual reality', it must be said that the mystery of Israel is present in the Church and the mystery of Israel is present in the Jewish people. For Paul, the *remnant* is Israel. And the Jewish people *is* also Israel. And when he warns the Gentile-Christian that the fate of the broken branches (11.17) does not give him the right to boast at the expense of the remaining branches, which would be to despise his own roots, Paul is suggesting that every branch is connatural to the root; we cannot despise the one without despising the other. According to Paul, it was Israel who recognized in Jesus the object of its hope and it is Israel who continues to wait for her Messiah in Judaism. Later on, we shall look at some of the consequences to be drawn from this apparently contradictory (and perhaps ambivalent) situation which opens up much richer perspectives than anything that could be said about the 'two Israels'.[6]

---

[6] D. Judant, *Les Deux Israël. Essai sur le mystère du salut d'Israël selon l'économie des deux Testaments* (*The Two Israels: Essay on the Mystery of the Salvation of Israel According to the Economy of the Two Testaments*), in French (Paris: Cerf, 1960).

The Teaching of Romans 9–11: Perspectives for the Future

Such are some of the deductions that may be drawn from the way Paul viewed the situation of the Jews of his time. But his perspective reaches far beyond what could be seen in the year 57 CE. In stating that 'part of Israel had its mind hardened, but only until the Gentiles have wholly come in' (Rom. 11.25), the Epistle to the Romans opens onto a future which is first of all historical and not only eschatological. The permanence of the Israel–Gentiles duality which, according to Paul's teaching, is directly linked to the salvation of the Gentiles,[7] is presented as lasting until the final redemption.

The future that Paul writes about in the Epistle to the Romans is partly known to us as history; for its interpretation we can and must be helped by the epistle itself.

Two millennia of history have demonstrated first of all the spiritual vitality of the Jewish people, even after the destruction of the Temple. The 'branches that were cut off' have not died. The faith and hope of Israel have not been extinguished. The permanence of Judaism is a reality, which cannot reasonably be accounted for in terms of refusal, sin, faithlessness, nor even by explanations making appeal to religious sentiment only.

On their side, the Gentile-Christians have remained in large part pagan. Of course, there is no need to regret that the Gentiles kept their identity when they received the gospel or that they were able to express their Christian faith within their own cultures. To say that the Gentile-Christians have remained pagan is in no way to refuse to see the fruits of conversion and of holiness that the gospel has produced in the Gentiles. What we are, however, saying is that conversion to Christ has not brought along with it reconciliation with Israel. We cannot but suspect that where Paul wrote, 'There can be neither Jew nor Greek' (Gal. 3.28), the Gentile-Christian would interpret

---

[7] See above, pp. 26–30.

'There is no more Jew, there is only the Greek', and consider a culturally Graeco-Latin Christianity as the necessary fulfilment of the hope of Israel. History has shown that, when Paul put the Gentile-Christian on guard against any temptation of arrogance toward Israel, there were good grounds for his warning, a warning that has largely gone unheard. The persistence of anti-Semitism, or simply of indifference toward Israel within the Church, demonstrates that the reconciliation, which we claim has been given in the death of Christ, in fact remains a goal yet to be attained.

Already – Not Yet

The relationship of the Church to the Jewish people is therefore marked like everything to do with the theology of salvation with the double sign of *already* and *not yet*.

The Christian waits for him who has already come.[8] Raised up with Christ (Col. 3.1), he waits for the whole creation to be freed from its slavery to corruption (Rom. 8.21). And while recognizing that the kingdom of heaven is close at hand (Matt. 4.17), he prays unceasingly that the kingdom may come (Matt. 6.10). The reconciliation of Israel and the Gentiles is itself to be seen within the perspective of a fulfilment already given but also to be hoped for.

By recognizing in the death of Christ the salvific event that destroys the wall of separation and which is a foundation of unity, we affirm that Jews and Gentiles are already gathered together in one body (Eph. 2.16). And the first Christian community, in which the branches issued from the Gentiles came to be grafted onto the trunk of Israel, shows that this communion has in fact been realized. At the same time, the

[8] The New Testament never uses the term or notion of *return* for designating the Parousia. Cf. F.-X. Durrwell, *La Résurrection de Jésus, mystère du salut* (*The Resurrection of Jesus, Mystery of Salvation*), in French (Paris: Cerf, 10th edn, 1976), p. 105.

actual exteriority which remains and which Paul could already observe between Israel and the believing Gentiles, reminds us that this unity, already given, is still to come.

The permanence of Judaism therefore appears as linked to *time*. On this basis it is open to an interpretation that cannot be reduced to refusal or faithlessness.[9] Israel has been chosen to be the trustee of the promise until the time of the fulfilment; its mission remains as long as the plenitude of the fulfilment is still to come.

Within this time, already sanctified by the hope and prayers of Israel, the kingdom of God arose in Jesus Christ as an irruption of eternity. Access has been given to a salvation anticipated by faith, remaining as an object of hope for all those called by grace 'not only out of the Jews but out of the Gentiles too' (Rom. 9.24).

Interiority – Exteriority

The Church, therefore, is both intrinsic and extrinsic to Israel. The attitude of Christians has to take into account and respect both these apparently contradictory aspects of a single reality.

Interiority

The Church constitutes Israel's remnant and is intrinsic to Israel. There is no point in coming back to this matter at any length since Christian tradition has always been aware of it, even if in too exclusive a manner.

Identifying the Church with the remnant of Israel means, first of all, recognizing in Jesus the one in whom the vocation and mission of Israel are concentrated[10] and who is fully entitled

---

[9] Without wishing to avoid the question of knowing what relation sin has with time, in delaying the accomplishment ...

[10] See for example how Matthew applies Scripture's words on Israel to Christ: Matt. 2.15; 4.1–11.

to introduce the nations into the Covenant made with Abraham.

In receiving Christ, the Gentiles receive a Scripture that forms a single entity with Jesus. But this Scripture cannot itself be dissociated from an exegetical, liturgical and spiritual tradition with which it is at one. This tradition, closely allied to the New Testament, is needed to make Jesus, who is rooted within that tradition, fully intelligible. It is increasingly agreed today, for example, that the New Testament uses the term 'Scripture' not only of the biblical text, *stricto sensu*, but more widely, of Scripture together with a tradition of commentary that has continued to flower within living Judaism, its trustee. 'Who can deny the debt that the New Testament owes to this Bible *as interpreted*, rather than to a virgin *sola Scriptura* newly emerged intact from the hands of its authors?'[11] There is no doubt that in more than one case, the 'according to the Scriptures' of the New Testament refers less to the biblical text itself than to its traditional interpretation.[12] The importance of this fact is more than documentary. It is far more than just a matter for Bible scholars. The gospel that the Christian receives lives within a tradition which overflows the Christian patrimony on every side; the gospel cannot be isolated from this tradition without being mutilated. It would therefore be quite illusory to claim to be able to draw a line of demarcation separating off Christianity from the territory of its neighbouring religion. Besides, if we wanted to remove everything Jewish from Christianity, we would have to remove the Bible, Jesus, the New Testament, the Eucharist and the greater part of the liturgy . . .

---

[11] R. Le Deaut, Introduction to *Targum of the Pentateuch*, (Sources chrétiennes, 282; Paris: Cerf, 1981), pp. 14–15.

[12] The reference to the 'third day', concerning the resurrection of Christ (1 Cor. 15.4), for instance, can be explained only by holding in mind the commentary of the midrash on Gen. 22.4 which says specifically that the third day is that of the resurrection of the dead (*Genesis Rabba* 56.1).

Exteriority

Clearly, all this can be expressed only from within the interior of the Christian faith that knows Jesus to be the one who received the heritage and who is authorized to bring in the Gentiles. For its part, Judaism does not adopt Christian conceptions of Christ and his mission and therefore the relationship perceived by the Christian is not lived out reciprocally. However, it is in one and the same movement that the Christian realizes what he has received from the Jewish people and respects the way in which Judaism sees itself.

Furthermore, the fact that Israel does not recognize Jesus to be its Messiah is linked to the affirmation of its own identity with regard to the Gentiles and therefore with regard to a Church which is in fact massively composed of Gentiles. The lack of recognition of the Messiahship of Jesus and the affirmation of the identity of the Jewish people are two realities which, without being the same, cannot be dissociated from each other.

On both accounts, therefore, Israel and the Church remain extrinsic to each other. In their attitude toward the Jews, Christians have to take this situation, and all that follows from it, into account.

Christians cannot appeal to the logic of the 'heritage' as a basis for taking over the spiritual and liturgical traditions of the Jewish people. Recognition of Israel means recognition that these traditions belong to it and that it has not been dispossessed of them. Christians cannot claim a right to this patrimony on the grounds that Jesus has legitimately handed it over to them, forgetting that the patrimony belongs as their personal property to a Jewish people which continues just as legitimately to call itself *Israel* and to base its identity on its tradition.

Neither can the Christian ignore the fact that through this tradition Judaism expresses a faith, a hope and a spiritual experience not recognized in Christianity, or only partially so. We cannot act as if communion were total and reciprocal, or as if the tradition of the one expressed the faith of the other without, in attempting to search for unity, running the risk of causing misunderstandings. To utilize elements of Jewish tradition to express Christian faith and prayer through them implies a sort of disrespect toward the meaning given them by the people who elaborated them.

St Augustine turned the Jews into porters whose task was to carry books whose real meaning only the Christians understood. Today's Christians must not fall too easily into the habit of acting as authorized interpreters of another people's tradition.

Finally, the Gentile-Christian who appropriates the symbols by which today's Israel expresses its identity may be following all kinds of more or less conscious motivations stretching from the – questionable – expression of an authentic love for Israel and a desire for communication with his roots to a mere quest for spiritual exoticism. One should be aware that this attitude might reflect more or less subtly two temptations that need to be borne in mind. The first would be to substitute oneself for Israel in order to confess, in its stead and with its own signs, the Lordship of Jesus Christ. The second would be the wish to take over in some way the actual identity of the chosen people; this would ultimately amount to nothing but a resurgence of the ancient 'jealousy' that the election of Israel arouses in the Gentiles. These two temptations illustrate the extraordinary difficulty that the Christian may encounter in situating himself correctly in relation to the Jewish people of today. They demonstrate how very narrow the way is between indifference and an interest, the expression of which is not necessarily untainted.

Strictly speaking, the way is actually nothing less than needle-thin; the Christian wanting to take into account all the questions raised by the encounter with the Jewish people finds himself caught in the midst of an apparently insoluble tension, between apparently incompatible requirements which nevertheless must be met simultaneously. Acting as if the Church were extrinsic to Israel means emptying the Christian faith of its content – unless the Church become heir of an Israel which no longer exists, so that in killing the heir to seize his inheritance (cf. Matt. 21.38) we come to deny all real continuity between biblical Israel and the Jewish people of today. But acting as if the communion were total and reciprocal is to pitch oneself into misunderstandings and show lack of respect for what the people of Israel says of itself: yet another way of glorying at Israel's expense.

In other words, no extrinsic attitude can, by itself, express what the relation of the Christian to the Jewish people must be. No principle can, by itself, express the truth of a relation that must first of all be interior. We are not dealing here with a question of law but with a spiritual matter. For the situation just described is nothing but the reflection of the situation of Christ himself in relation to his people and in relation to the Gentiles: the tension simply cannot be abolished and only the Spirit can help us accept a situation originating in Christ, a situation which can be lived only in him.

Conclusion

The Church attains self-understanding and self-definition by appropriating the memory and hope of Israel as these are realized and manifested in the liturgy. But Israel is not merely anterior to the Church. Its destiny is not simply to be a prefiguration. We cannot endow terms like 'people, Covenant', and all the fundamental notions by which the Church expresses her identity, with their full meaning simply by an exegesis of texts. The Church has acquired her self-understanding through the spiritual experience of a people whose permanence is the living sign that the gifts of God are irrevocable (Rom. 11.29).

The Jewish people after Christ continues to appear as the reference point by which the Church of the Gentiles defines herself without, however, being able to identify with this people. This otherness is ambiguous, as already noted; it involves the indissoluble continuation of the affirmation of the identity of a people with its refusal to accept the Messiahship of Jesus. Is this linkage essential? Christian thinking has accorded too little attention to this question up to now to make it possible to do more than give a hint of an answer. It is enough to observe that Paul, faced with the fact that Israel as a people did not accept the gospel, was not satisfied with the explanation of 'faithlessness'. When he referred to what he called, with the vocabulary available to him, 'a hardening of a part of Israel', it was to fall in adoration before a plan of God beyond his comprehension ...

Therefore – and this is not the least of paradoxes – Israel appears more clearly, in its very refusal, as 'the *other*', a people set aside so that through it, a blessing will descend on all the families of the earth. Election and setting aside remain, for the Christian, the permanent sign of the free gift which makes him what he is: that which comes by way of the other, comes from the Other.

APPENDIX

People, Land and State

Concerning the Recognition of the State of Israel by the Holy See

The *Fundamental Agreement* signed on 30 December 1993 between the Holy See and the State of Israel has been greeted, with good reason, as an event of primary importance in the history of the relations between the Catholic Church and the Jews.[1] A more thorough examination shows that things are not as simple as they appear at first sight. The following lines aim to open up avenues of thought on certain aspects of a particularly complex subject.

This complexity derives essentially from the difficulty of clearly defining who the partners are and what the object of the Agreement is.

The partners. The vagueness of the vocabulary used in press reports reflects this complexity. Certain reports speak of the recognition of Israel by the *Church*, others of an agreement between two *States* (Israel and the Vatican). Who is the 'recognizing' body from the Catholic side? The Church? The mini-State of the Vatican? In reality the signatory is neither one nor the other, but the Holy See. The introduction of this third element, though indispensable, does not of itself bring the clarity required; it presupposes fairly subtle distinctions which are beyond most people's grasp and which add to the complexity of the question. The same ambiguity is found, if

---

[1] The original text can be obtained in ORIGINS 23/30 (Washington, DC: Catholic News Service, 13 January 1994), pp. 525–8.

in a somewhat lesser degree on the side of the other partner. Here again, the identity of the signatory is clearly indicated, it is the State of Israel. But this state, even if no different in any way, at least legally, from other members of the international community, is not quite a state like all others: most Jews, the majority of whom are not Israeli, have more or less strong links with the State of Israel, and although the nature of these links is hard to define, they are largely 'religious' even though the term requires very careful definition in our context.

The actual terms of the Agreement do not eliminate these ambiguities: according to the text the partners are '*the Holy See and the State of Israel*' but the grounds of the Agreement as enumerated in the preamble refer to 'the unique nature of the friendship between the *Catholic Church and the Jewish people*'. The ensuing text recognizes implicitly the existence of a special link between the State of Israel and the Jewish people in its entirety, for it specifies that 'the Holy See takes this opportunity to reiterate its condemnation of hatred, persecution and all other manifestations of anti-Semitism directed against the Jewish people and individual Jews anywhere, at any time and by anyone'.[2] Are we to understand that the State of Israel is considered here as representing the whole of the Jewish people? In what sense and within what limits?[3]

A certain element of ambiguity remains when the object of the Agreement is examined. On the Jewish side, there is willingness to give the event theological significance: the Agreement of 30 December is to be regarded as the Church's recognition of the particular character of the bond between the

---

[2] Article 2,2. The formulation of this article is strongly inspired by the Conciliar Declaration *Nostra Aetate* no. 4, on relations between the Church and non-Christian religions (paragraph 4, on Judaism).

[3] The question can be extended: if we accept that the State of Israel represents the Jewish People over against the confessional partner represented by the Holy See, where, in this context, are Judaism and the rabbinate? (Totally absent from the Agreement of 30 December except for general allusions to freedom of religion and of conscience in article 1,2 and condemnation of the profanation of synagogues in article 2,2).

people of Israel and the Land of Israel as based on the biblical revelation. A number of Catholics interpret the text in the same vein while others, on the contrary, stress its exclusively diplomatic character. As to the actual text of the Agreement, it says simply that the two signatories are 'mindful of the particular character and universal significance of the Holy Land'. It should also be noted that in this document, which marks the implicit recognition of the State of Israel by the Holy See, the word 'recognize' is used several times, most often to say that the State of Israel recognizes the right of the Catholic Church to carry on her proper activities and support her institutions in the Holy Land.

The ambiguities are reflections of the asymmetry affecting the relation between the Jewish people and the Catholic Church.

Dispersed among the nations, the Jewish people has always nursed an aspiration for 'a national existence in this land'.[4] This desire is founded on the promise made to Abraham by God (Gen. 15.18) and constantly recalled by the prophets (Ezek. 36.17–38 etc.). It combines what we call the 'religious' and the 'political' in a way that has no equivalent on the Christian side. A document, which the Holy See addressed in 1985 to preachers and to catechists, invited Catholics to 'understand this religious attachment, which has deep roots in biblical tradition'.[5] The text added immediately that although Christians were invited to 'understand' this attachment, they were not thereby obliged to 'accept a particular religious interpretation of this relationship'.

---

[4] 'L'attitude des chrétiens à l'égard du judaïsme'. ('The Attitude of Christians towards Judaism'). Statement by the French Bishops' Committee for Relations with Jews, April 1973. Translated from French in Croner (ed.) *Stepping Stones*, p. 60.

[5] Notes on the Correct Way to Present the Jews and Judaism in Preaching and Catechesis in the Roman Catholic Church, 24 June 1985. In Croner (ed.), *More Stepping Stones*. There is a commentary on this text entitled: *Juifs et chrétiens, un nouveau regard* (*Jews and Christians, a new look*). See Foreword, n. 1.

The State of Israel is considered by many Jews as the start of the realization of the biblical promise of the ingathering on the land promised to the Patriarchs – but here again we must be careful not to simplify a complicated reality.

This reality has no equivalent on the Christian side. Dispersed in 'Greek or barbarian cities according to the destiny of each', says the Epistle to Diognetus, Christians have no aspirations to be gathered into a state of their own. The 'flesh' of the Church is composed of men and women, each one a citizen of his own country. The Church is not a state among those existing in the world and the Holy See is not equivalent or homologous to the Israeli government.[6] The Vatican State, which constitutes a useful means for guaranteeing the political independence of the Holy See, is in no way a counterpart of the State of Israel. It is the legal inheritor of the Papal States of the Middle Ages and does not embody in any way some kind of aspiration on the part of Christian peoples to be gathered into a sovereign state distinct from other nations!

Both the imprecision in the vocabulary of the commentators, and the presence within the Agreement itself of several relatively vague formulations, show how impossible it is for the Church and for Israel to find common ground on which the two partners could situate themselves rigorously at the same level. This asymmetry, and the difficulty that the Catholic side has in defining itself in relation to the Jewish side, is far from being ecclesiologically insignificant.

The questions raised by the Agreement of 30 December have as much to do with the understanding that the Church has of herself as with her perception of Jewish reality. In my opinion, it is of the highest significance that, in her encounter with the

---

[6] The Fundamental Agreement (Art. 11.2) makes it clear that 'the Holy See, while maintaining in every case the right to exercise its moral and spiritual teaching-office, deems it opportune to recall that, owing to its own character, it is solemnly committed to remaining a stranger to all merely temporal conflicts, which principle applies specifically to disputed territories and unsettled borders.'

Jewish people, the Church is here once again forced to ask herself about her own identity and about her relations with the world and society. If the Holy See is purely and simply identified with the Church, what can be the meaning of the diplomatic recognition of a state by the Church?[7] If we do make a distinction between them, on what basis is it to be? How is the Church committed, or not committed, by a diplomatic act of the Holy See?

New questions arise when we come to what constitutes the object of the recognition. Is the establishment of diplomatic relations with the State of Israel any different from recognition of any other state? If we answer in the affirmative, it means that this state is not, for the Church, a state like the others. Should we then say that the Church recognizes (but in what sense?) the significance that the Jewish people gives to its own ingathering in the land of its ancestors and that she also accepts the significance that the existence of a sovereign state has in this context? But if the answer is negative, what is the meaning of the phrase in the preamble referring to the unique nature of the relations between the Catholic Church and the Jewish people? Answers given by Catholics to each one of these points cover the entire spectrum of possibilities.[8]

This complexity explains why it is possible to interpret the impact of the Agreement in many diverse ways.

---

[7] It must be remembered that a given person can be a member of the Church and citizen of a state at one and the same time. This is evidence that the two affiliations are not of the same order and that the two realities cannot be put on the same level. The Constitution *Lumen Gentium*, the most recent dogmatic exposition concerning the Church, says nothing about papal diplomacy (and let it be said in passing that the word 'Vatican' is not to be found in the index of the acts of the last Council!). It is very hard to make the uninitiated, even when they are Catholic, understand that these institutions do not belong to the nature of the Church ...

[8] In practice, the Agreement of 30 December and its echoes in the press had the effect of revealing to many people that the Holy See had not yet recognized Israel, even though the great majority of the public, even Catholics, had assumed that the recognition had been accorded long before, or had never even wondered about it.

From the juridical point of view, we are talking about diplomatic recognition between two bodies in international law, as embodied in an exchange of ambassadors. Even if the precaution is taken to speak in this context of *Holy See* rather than of *Vatican*, acts of papal diplomacy are not declarations of the Magisterium. Neither are they disciplinary decisions binding on the consciences of the faithful, given that the faithful are allowed to exercise freedom of choice in political matters. We need to remember that the theological position of the Church with relation to the Jewish people, was defined by Vatican II in its declaration on the non-Christian religions. In terms of its content, the Agreement of 30 December 1993 is much closer to a concordat than to a doctrinal declaration.

But this juridical point of view does not express the whole symbolic significance of the Agreement. For Jews as well as for those Christians who are attentive to the evolution of relations between the Church and the Jewish people, it appears as a sign of an important change of attitude on the part of the ecclesiastical authorities. The extent of this change should not be overestimated in case it should cause misunderstanding and disappointment, but that a change has taken place does appear to be real. It was in fact hard not to notice that the non-recognition of the State of Israel by the Holy See was at one with a long tradition having its roots in centuries-old teaching. The Fathers of the Church believed they could affirm that the exile of the Jewish people from its land was the punishment of the Jews, that it demonstrated the obsolescence of the first covenant and that it was therefore definitive: 'Until the end of the world [the Jewish people] has lost the independence of the destroyed city' (St Hilary of Poitiers); 'The Jews will never return to their ancient state' (St John Chrysostom); 'The desolation of the Jews will last until the end of the world' (St Jerome). And when the Father of modern Zionism, Theodore Herzl, went to visit Pius X at the Vatican in 1904 to describe his plan for the establishment of a Jewish national home in Palestine, it was for theological reasons of the same order that the Pope refused to help: 'The Jews should have been the first to recognize Christ. They have not done it yet'. Until quite recently, the Holy See was using arguments of this type to justify its continuing refusal to support the project of the creation of a Jewish State.

It is easy to understand that many observers have assessed the Agreement of December 1993 in the light of this past, ancient and recent, and their assessment is therefore sensitive to the change of attitude demonstrated in the Agreement. Though care must be taken not to confuse the different levels in a particularly complex domain, and to avoid taking up emotional positions on a subject in which sensitivities are sharper than elsewhere, it must be admitted that this agreement represents an important stage on the long road which will lead Jews and Christians to a better understanding of each other.

Bibliography

Aletti, J.-N. *Comment Dieu est-il juste?* Paris: Seuil, 1991.

Beauchamp, P. *L'un et l'autre testament*. Paris: Seuil, 1976.

Beauchamp, P. *Le récit, la lettre et le corps*. Paris: Cerf, 1982.

Blumenkranz, B. *Juifs et chrétiens dans le monde occidental (430–1096)*. La Haye: Mouton, 1960.

Bonnard, P.-E. *Le second Isaïe, son disciple et leurs editeurs. Isaïe 40–66*. Paris: Gabalda, 1972.

Borowitz, E. B. *How can a Jew speak of faith today?* Philadephia: Westminster Press, 1969.

Bouyer, L. *Le Trône de la Sagesse. Essai sur la signification du culte marial*. Paris: Cerf, 1957.

Brunot, A. *Homélies pour l'année A. Dimanches et fêtes*. Mulhouse: Salvator, 1977

Brunot, A. *Homélies pour l'année B. Dimanches et fêtes*. Mulhouse: Salvator, 1978.

Brunot, A. *Nouvelles homélies pour l'année. A*. Mulhouse: Salvator, 1980.

Cerbelaud, D. *Ecouter Israël*. Paris: Cerf, 1995.

Croner, H. *Stepping Stones to further Jewish-Christian Relations*. London and New York: Stimulus Books, 1977.

Croner, H. *More stepping stones*. New York: Paulist Press, 1985.

Duquoc, C. *Jésus, homme libre. Esquisse d'une christologie*. Paris: Cerf, 1981

Durrwell, F.-X. *La Résurrection de Jésus, mystère du salut*. 10th Edition. Paris: Cerf, 1976.

Fackenheim, E. L. *God's presence in history: Jewish Affirmations and Philosophical Reflections*. New York: Harper & Row, 1970

Fisher E. and L. Klenicki. *In Our time: the Flowering of Jewish-Catholic Dialogue*. New York: Paulist/Stimulus Press, 1990.

Fleishner, E. *Auschwitz, Beginning of a New Era? Reflexions on the Holocaust*. New York: KTAV Publishing House, 1977.

Flusser, D. *Jésus.* French translation with a foreword by B. Dupuy. Paris: Seuil, 1970.

Flusser, D. in collaboration with R. Steven Notley. *Jesus.* English translation. Jerusalem: The Magnes Press, 1997.

Harkins, P. W. *Saint John Chrysostom. Discourses against Judaizing Christians.* Washington, D.C.: The Catholic University of America Press, 1979.

Herford, R. T. *Pirke Aboth. The Ethics of the Talmud: Sayings of the Fathers. Text, complete translation and commentaries.* New York: Schocken, 1962.

Heschel, A. *The earth is the Lord's.* Woodstock, Vermont: Jewish Lights, 1995.

Hoch, M.-T. and Dupuy, B. *Les Églises devant le judaïsme. Documents officiels 1948–1978. Textes rassemblés, traduits et annotés.* Paris: Cerf, 1980.

International Catholic-Jewish Liaison Committee. *Fifteen years of Catholic-Jewish Dialogue, 1970–1985.* Rome: Libreria Editrice Laterense and Vaticana, 1988.

Judant, D. *Les Deux Israël. Essai sur le mystère du salut d'Israël selon l'économie des deux Testaments.* Paris: Cerf, 1960.

Judant, D. *Judaïsme et Christianisme. Dossier Patristique* Paris: Cèdre, 1969.

Laurentin, R. *L'Eglise et les juifs à Vatican II.* Tournai: Casterman, 1967.

Le Deaut, R. 'Introduction' to *Targum of the Pentateuch*, Vol. V. Paris: Cerf, 1984.

Lovsky, F. *Antisémitisme et mystère d'Israel.* Paris: Albin Michel, 1955.

Lovsky, F. *La déchirure de l'absence.* Paris: Calmann-Lévy, 1971.

Maritain, J. *Le mystère d'Israel et autres essais.* Paris: Desclée de Brouwer, 1965.

Marrus, C. R. and R. O. Paxton. *Vichy France and the Jews.* New York: Basic Books, 1981.

Missel Emmaus des dimanches. Paris: Desclée de Brouwer, 1979.

Missel Emmaus. Lectionnaire de semaine. In 10 vols. Paris: Desclée de Brouwer, 1980.

Mussner, Franz. *Tractate on the Jews. The significance of Judaism for Christian Faith.* English translation and with a foreword by

Leonard Swidler. Phildelphia: Fortress Press; London: SPCK, 1984.

Neher, A. *The exile of the word: from the silence of the Bible to the silence of Auschwitz.* English translation by D. Maisel. Philadelphia: Jewish Publication Society of America, 1981.

Neubauer, A. and Driver, S. R. *The fifty-third chapter of Isaiah according to the Jewish interpreters.* 2 vols. New York: KTAV Publishing House, 1969.

Nobecourt, J. *Le 'Vicaire' et l'histoire.* Paris: Seuil, 1964.

Osterreicher, J. M. *Anatomy of Contempt. A Critique of R.R. Ruether's 'Faith and Fratricide'.* South Orange, NJ: The Institute of Judeo-Christian Studies, Seton Hall University, 1975.

Pawlikowski, J. *Jesus and the Theology of Israel.* Wilmington: Michael Glazier, 1989.

Poliakov, L. *History of Anti-Semitism.* 4 vols. English translation. New York: Vanguard, 1976.

Remaud, M. *Chrétiens et juifs entre le passé et l'avenir.* Brussels: Editions Lessius, 2000.

Rubenstein, R. L. *After Auschwitz. Radical theology and contemporary Judaism.* New York: The Bobbs-Merrill Company, Inc., 1966.

Ruether, R. R. *Faith and Fratricide. The theological roots of anti-Semitism.* New York: Seabury Press, 1974.

Remaud, M. *Chrétiens et Juifs entre le passé et l'aveni.* Brussels: Editions Lessius, 2000.

Schubert, K. *Jésus à la lumière du judaïsme du premier siècle.* French translation from German by A. Liefooghe. Paris: Cerf, 1974.

Shermis, M. and Zannoni, A. eds.: *Introduction to Jewish-Christian Relations.* New York: Paulist Press, 1991.

Simon, M. *Verus Israel: A study on relations between Christians and Jews in the Roman Empire.* English translation by H. McKeating. New York: Oxford University Press, 1986.

Wiesel, E. *Night.* English translation by Stella Rodway. New York: Hill and Wang, 1960.

Wiesel, E. *Célébration biblique.* Paris: Seuil, 1975.

Williamson, C. M. *A Guest in the House of Israel: Post-Holocaust Church Theology.* Louisville: Westminster/John Knox Press, 1993.

Biblical Citations

Old Testament

Genesis
2.24   11
12.3   62, 121
22.4   133

Exodus
4.22   13, 23
31.14   118
34   120

Leviticus
19.2   113
19.18   14
19.37   38

Numbers
24.17   99

Deuteronomy
32.15   56

Joshua
24   120

2 Kings
22–23   120

2 Chronicles
34   120

Nehemiah
9–10   120

Job
13.15   73

Psalms
22   72
22.8   23
40.7   113
91.12   71
119.3, 17, 142   113

Isaiah
41.8–9   26
42.1   59
43.10   26
44.1–2, 21   26
45.4   26
48.20   26
49.3   13, 26
52.14–15   60
53   21, 60
53.3   44
53.10   87
53.11   25
53.12   20
53.4   20
53.8   23

Jeremiah
31.31-4   120

Ezekiel
36.26-7   120
37.3   71

Habakkuk
2.4   118

Zechariah
12.10   38

New Testament

Matthew
1.1–17   120
2.15   132
3.15   23
4.1–11   132
4.17   131
5.17   17
5.48   113
6.10   131
7.24–7   92
8.17   21
13.53–8   110
14.28–31   71
21.38   136
23.1-12   100
23.16-22   96
25.4   67
27.46–50   24

Mark
6.1-6   110

Luke
1.54   26
3.23–38   120
4.16–30   110, 114
22.37   21
23.34   46
24.27   115

John
1.14   114
2.24   95
4.22   12, 122
12.38   21
17.11   10

Acts
2.14-36   115
6.7   114
9.8   5
8.34   21

12.24   114
19.20   114
22.11   5
26.22   17

Romans
5.10   28
8.21   76, 131
9–11   6, 27-30, 32, 33, 37, 49, 59,
        77, 78, 123-31, 132
11.15   13, 27
11.33–6   58
15.21   21

1 Corinthians
10.1–11   120

2 Corinthians
1.20   63
3.16   38
4.16   120
5.21   27

Galatians
3.28   11
4.4   63

Ephesians
1.13   114
2–3   6, 33, 37
2.14   10, 78
2.16   131
3.6   114, 126
5.32   11
3.1–11   11
5.31   11
2.15   11

Colossians
3.1   131
3.10   120

Index of Names

Index of Subjects